Settling America

The Ethnic Expression of 14 Contemporary Poets

Settling America

The Ethnic Expression of

14 Contemporary Poets

Edited by David Kherdian

Macmillan Publishing Co., Inc.
New York

811.08
K
C.2

10   9   8   7   6   5   4   3   2   1

Library of Congress Cataloging in Publication Data
Kherdian, David, comp. Settling America.
1. American Poetry—20th century. 2. Minorities
—United States—Poetry. [1. American poetry—20th
century. 2. Minorities—Poetry] I. Title.
PS615.K5   811'.5'408   74–8128
ISBN 0–02–750240–6

Thanks are due to the following for permission to include copyrighted
poems:

Joy Harjo for her "The Lost Weekend bar," "Creek Mother Poem," "Lame
Deer," "Ignacio, Colorado," "Snake Poem I," "(A Hopi Woman Talking),"
and "The People," Copyright © 1974 by Joy Harjo.

Luís Omar Salinas for his "Ode to Mexican Experience," "Happiness Is
a Charlie Chaplin Movie," "This Is Not a Poem," "Ode to a Violin,"
"Barefoot," "For the Waiter at Jhonny Pavlovs," "What a Way to Lose
the War" and "Whats My Name If Not Everyone Elses," Copyright © 1974
by Luís Omar Salinas.

Mei Berssenbrugge for "Chronicles: Numbers One and Two," "Chronicles:
Number Three," "El Bosco," "Book of the Dead, Prayer 14," "Fish and
Swimmers and Lonely Birds Sweep Past Us," "Abortion," "Propeller
Sleep," "In Bhaudanath," "Spirit," and "Old Man Let's Go Fishing in
the Yellow Reeds of the Bay," Copyright © 1974 by Mei Berssenbrugge.

Black Sparrow Press for "In Split: Diocletian's Palace" by Stephen
Stepanchev from his A MAN RUNNING IN THE RAIN, Copyright © 1969
by Stephen Stepanchev; "Buying Lilies," "Irondale," "Voyage," and "The
Roads" by Stephen Stepanchev from his THE MAD BOMBER, Copyright ©
1972 by Stephen Stepanchev.

Preface

No one is as obsessed with America as the sons and daughters of immigrants, excepting, perhaps, those of us who were here first: the Indians; or—for as long or nearly as long as the original settlers—the Blacks.

In youth, a time not meant for decision-making, those foreign-feeling youngsters are given the toughest choice of all—to choose between the culture of the street and that of the home. Between wanting to be accepted and not being able to, between rejecting the father and then America, and not being able to, bitterness drives the child inward to his only home.

The real problems come later, when choices lead to decisions that become a way of life—for the arguments of the mind are soon met with the demands of the blood that reassert their claim and, more than the mind, determine the course of our future life. This is the ground to which the poet holds his ear, clinging to the snags and traumas that will determine the direction of his becoming art.

Art is no more than life, stealing its energy from the base and forlorn hopes of man. Those for whom language is being, the only construct possible out of which to deal with life and ultimately bend it to the will we impose on experience—our interpretation of it, our ability to change it for ourselves and for everyone else—soon learn that sorrow makes for singing; that with our father's fire and our own mud, one more attempt at grace and the resolution of wrong is possible through the form of art.

The obvious theme of this book is America, into and out of whose gut more men have been chewed, swallowed, shat and then forgotten, than in any other civilization or time. It takes a force as strong as greed (which melted down ore and men in her westward-pointing foundries) to make the individual's claim for oneself stick and hold in a land that has never stood still for anyone. The strongest, most insistent, have been able to do here what was never possible anywhere else: know themselves, name their suffering and claim it in a poem—to be handed to the next runner in the endless race for truth, honor, dignity and pride.

Obviously, all of this makes for difficult art; the dichotomy of cultures, the urgency for utterance, all the great confusions to be set right, can bring to the poem almost more experience than the traditional poem is accustomed to taking upon itself. But this book makes clear that only a need as great as that felt by each of these particular poets can make for vital and urgent art.

The uncommon in America has become the ordinary, and while the minority experience shifts and enlarges, it has now given to all of us, in these poems, a feeling that we are participants of the one drama, and that it is the people closest to the heart of it who are best qualified to give us their reports— which are our lives.

DAVID KHERDIAN

Malden Bridge, N.Y.
December 16, 1973

Contents

Settling America

The Ethnic Expression of 14 Contemporary Poets

Mei Berssenbrugge

Mei Berssenbrugge was born in Peking in 1947, the first grand-child of a solid academic family. Her mother is Chinese and her father American of Dutch descent. She left China with her mother at the age of nine months for Berkeley, California, where her father finished school. She grew up there, in Cambridge and then in Framingham, Massachusetts, a suburban New England community with very few Chinese, so her experience of China comes mostly through the stories her mother has told her, repeated and polished through the years.

She studied writing at Reed College and Columbia University. She reads Shakespeare, Rilke, Whitman and Vallejo, dislikes poetry in translation and advises against too much school for poets, knowing this from experience.

Her adult life has been spent on the move—Nepal, Pakistan, New York City and Juneau, Alaska. She now lives in an adobe house in northern New Mexico, which she calls a "land of beer cans, churches, mountains and cars, where a pick-up car plows into your house at midday on a dead straight road."

A pamphlet of her poems, FISH SOULS (1971), was published in a limited edition. The Greenfield Review Press published her first full-length book, SUMMITS MOVE WITH THE TIDE, in 1974.

MEI BERSSENBRUGGE WRITES: *I wonder what being an ethnic writer means, and if that is what I am, I've given up telling stories about my Chinese relatives; even the stories of loss have passed from me as a subject, though I don't forget them. My poems now about a search for spirit, wherever I can find it.*

CHRONICLES: NUMBERS ONE AND TWO

My father hurried
two thousand miles
across that great lumbering back
of China
to catch up with my mother
who had lit out;
he stopped short at
the oriental moongate,
peered at plum blossoms
creeping over the high wall
and did not knock:
he gave his message to a rickshaw boy
with a foolish grin.

My Chinese grandfather
survived a mule trek first-hand,
a steam ship journey
to Cambridge, Massachusetts
in 1910;
he wanted to do some
mission work
at Harvard College;
he roomed with a widow and three
hoop-skirted daughters on Mount Auburn Street
and went home
with a taste for apple pie.

CHRONICLES: NUMBER THREE

I was born the year of the loon
in a great commotion. My mother—
who used to pack $500 cash
in the shoulders of her fur gambling coat,
who had always considered herself

the family's "First Son"—
took one look at me
and lit out again
for a vacation to Sumatra.
Her brother purchased my baby clothes;
I've seen them, little clown suits,
of silk and color.

Each day
my Chinese grandmother bathed me
with elaboration in an iron tub;
amahs waiting in lines
with sterilized water and towels
clucked and smiled
and rushed about the tall stone room
in tiny slippers.

After my grandfather
accustomed himself
to this betrayal by First Son,
he would take me in his arms,
walk with me
by the plum trees, cherries, persimmons;
he showed me the stiff robes
of my ancestors and their drafty hall,
the long beards of his learned old friends,
and his crickets.

Grandfather talked to me, taught me.
At two months, my mother tells me,
I could sniff for flowers,
stab my small hand upwards to moon.
Even today I get proud
when I remember
this all took place in Chinese.

EL BOSCO

for Hieronymus Bosch

If you offer your bag of butterflies,
seek honey, talk with a loon's head,
if you push fruit like a reptile up the mountain,
eat sprigs of rue from the cock's tail,
weep on your knees by the swan trail
like an angel or a goatherd,
if you cower in your crooked shack, awaiting
the small cherry-colored birds,
if you mourn,
despise skulls,
beat sinners like beggars,
hide manuscripts in the hollow of your foot
you'll still die;
even if you scathed your face with earthly jagged light,
even if you swept a little home for yourself
in a broken jug.

BOOK OF THE DEAD, PRAYER 14

Good-bye,
try to stay awake now you're dead.
Look hard at those demons
and don't be afraid.
All the bright lights and bells
are yourself returning
from wandering.
Try to look at them.
What terrifies
you must be beautiful.
I won't cry, make you sad.

If you embrace
these assaults you'll be free.
But of course you are frightened.
Hair stiffens
all over you. So you'll fall
back down to us, back
into another dying body.
So I'll see you again.
Maybe without knowing you,
also knowing.
I tell you so you won't worry.
Try to stay awake.

FISH AND SWIMMERS AND LONELY BIRDS SWEEP PAST US

Today I love you so much I mistrust you—
our future bows out and swells
like liquid and falls under a bird's wing

each day runs after the other days
joining them with its tiny body
and heartbeats

our bodies
lean toward center when we walk
sealed in a floating bell
phosphorus lighting up our eyes

and the bell is ringing
fish and swimmers
and lonely birds sweep by all around us

—and I look at you and you're invisible

5 / MEI BERSSENBRUGGE

ABORTION

When we walked outside at sunset
a tenement was burning to the ground
water tore bricks from the walls
and ashes fell in my hair
I wore your big goosedown jacket
and hugged my sleeves watching
from behind a playground fence
the rampant light

PROPELLER SLEEP

I've learned to recognize angels
riding the city busses
in their white T shirts
by their utterly plain faces

Their flesh
which is human almost
shifts to air at its frontiers

Their shadows
are casual shapes their friends wear
the unfleshed dreams accompanying them
across the vapor lamps

Angels beat their wings
so we won't forget them
They grieve
at being born of men and not angels
Even if one stays by your side seven years
it is a parallel flight

IN BHAUDANATH

If your eyes fall
let them
if the thigh bone
takes off and hollows out
it makes
a good flute

if your shining
amber skull
fills with liquid
you know

it is clean
water
from the mountains.

SPIRIT

This straw horse and this crabshell
and this Peruvian gold man,
these prayer beads with silver
bell and dorje,
the dried mushrooms,
the bone flute you carved
are my birdhouses
for souls.

In a fishbowl terrarium it rains;
green softens, breaks out of stems
into eyes, breath.

Let my oldest thought
be a crack: I am
tongues.

OLD MAN LET'S GO FISHING
IN THE YELLOW REEDS OF THE BAY

Our flat bottomed boat
glides through the reeds of the bay.
Seagulls fly up huge and raucous.
Ducks turn their bottoms up in the mire.

Their litter of clamshells and horsecrab
on the sand proves them better fishermen,
but we fish the whole afternoon.
The sun on its own line pulls slowly down.
Red tomatoes on our bait-can turn gold.

I've made drawings
of grass streaming in the wind,
and you, straw hat, full suspenders,
eyes lost in thick spectacles listening to birds.

I would draw you now
if my two dreaming hands
were not caught happily in yours.

Gregory Corso

Gregory Corso was born March 26, 1930, on Bleecker Street in New York's Greenwich Village, of an Italian immigrant mother and a first generation Italian-American father. He was sentenced to jail as a teen-ager and it was there that he was first introduced to books and poetry. The experience was so profound that years later he was able to dedicate his book GASOLINE ". . . to the angels of Clinton Prison who, in my 17th year, handed me, from all the cells surrounding me, books of illumination." After his release from prison he met Allen Ginsberg, who encouraged his gift for writing. Ginsberg's vitality and Corso's rambunctious spirit catalyzed the Beat Movement that permanently altered American poetry.

Although his education stopped with grade school, he eventually acquired the equivalent of two years of college by sneaking into English classes at Yale University, where he learned to love Shelley. It was at Yale, too, where he had written his first original poems, that in 1955 friends of the young poet published his first book, THE VESTAL LADY OF BRATTLE.

He has worked as a manual laborer, reporter (for the *Los Angeles Examiner*), merchant seaman and college instructor. He has traveled extensively in the United States and abroad, and has always written out of these experiences. His one marriage ended in divorce. He is the father of two daughters.

Gregory Corso has written five books of poems, a novel and several plays. His major publishers are City Lights Books and New Directions.

GREGORY CORSO WRITES: *When I am ready for the happy hunting ground I doubt I'll feel that I have missed something. Poetry has been to me what a coal miner's hat is to him; it enabled me to light up the dark ahead, to see, and to pray that I may light up that darkness and so justify its ways to men and to God.*

IN THE FLEETING HAND OF TIME

On the steps of the bright madhouse
I hear the bearded bell shaking down the woodlawn
the final knell of my world
I climb and enter a firey gathering of knights
they unaware of my presence lay forth sheepskin plans
and with mailcoated fingers trace my arrival
back back back when on the black steps of Nero lyre Rome
        I stood
in my arms the wailing philosopher
the final call of mad history
Now my presence is known
my arrival marked by illuminated stains
The great windows of Paradise open
Down to radiant dust fall the curtains of Past Time
In fly flocks of multicolored birds
Light winged light O the wonder of light
Time takes me by the hand
born March 26 1930 I am led 100 mph o'er the vast market
        of choice
what to choose? what to choose?
Oh————and I leave my orange room of myth
no chance to lock away my toys of Zeus
I choose the room of Bleecker Street
A baby mother stuffs my mouth with a pale Milanese breast
I suck I struggle I cry O Olympian mother
unfamiliar this breast to me
Snows
Decade of icy asphalt doomed horses
Weak dreams Dark corridors of P.S.42 Roofs Ratthroated
        pigeons
Led 100 mph over these all too real Mafia streets
profanely I shed my Hermean wings
O Time be merciful

throw me beneath your humanity of cars
feed me to giant grey skyscrapers
exhaust my heart to your bridges
I discard my lyre of Orphic futility

And for such betrayal I climb these bright mad steps
and enter this room of paradiscal light
ephemeral
Time
a long long dog having chased its orbited tail
comes grabs my hand
and leads me into conditional life

THREE

1

The streetsinger is sick
crouched in the doorway, holding his heart.

One less song in the noisy night.

2

Outside the wall
the aged gardener plants his shears
A new young man
has come to snip the hedge

3

Death weeps because Death is human
spending all day in a movie when a child dies.

When I think back to grammar school
I am overcome with breathlessness and sweet feeling—
Freighted to that glorious mahogany time
when bluecoats cheered each other with pewter mugs
and snow-hunched sentries eyed young Washington dismount
and Indians covered their horses with Algonquin rugs
Where perhaps a goodly witch buying sassafras
rubbed shoulders with Ben Franklin picking
        half-pennies from a tiny purse—

I played Christopher Columbus aged ten
in the great assembly hall before all
and I clearly remember as I sat
dreamily on the docks of Genoa
the beautiful picture of Washington at Valley Forge
Quite disastrous that
because when Queen Isabella asked my name
I said George

I learned in grammar school
that Lincoln walked many miles for a book
which he read lying on his stomach
        before a bubbling-kettle fireplace
That's how I wanted to read a book!
So as soon as the class was over
I hurried a mile from my neighborhood library
        to another library
Of course they wouldn't issue me a card
"Use the library in your own neighborhood"
So I stole my book
and late that night

under my blanket with a little flashlight
I read
And I do not exaggerate when I say
I fully felt the joy that was Lincoln's

It was the fourth grade when the teacher
took us to Trinity Church to see
Alexander Hamilton's grave—
Carmine wanted to laugh
The way he laughed made me laugh
And the way we laughed made the whole class laugh
He did that at the Planetarium
and because of it the teacher denied us the stars
When I was young I was able to be serious if I wanted
I did not laugh
He made funny faces
        scratched himself in dirty places
He did his utmost to deny me Hamilton
With all my might I listened to what the teacher
had to say about a man whose life I hold in high esteem

I never cared much about Patrick Henry
and Paul Revere too
Nor was there anything about the redcoats I liked
They were the enemy
no different from the Germans and the Japs
        I was a year later taught to hate
Yet one redcoat there was
        made me see the majesty of the English
It was the death of General Wolfe
the biggest picture in the school
The battle was in full force
war at its loveliest
and he lay there
        dying in the arms of soldiers

I'd a D conduct in that school
Never the tack on the teacher's chair
but oh, I was bad when I was bad

THE LAST GANGSTER

Waiting by the window
my feet enwrapped with the dead bootleggers of Chicago
I am the last gangster, safe, at last,
waiting by a bullet-proof window.

I look down the street and know
the two torpedoes from St. Louis.
I've watched them grow old
. . . guns rusting in their arthritic hands.

THE LAST WARMTH OF ARNOLD

Arnold, warm with God,
hides beneath the porch
remembering the time of escape, imprisoned in Vermont,
shoveling snow. Arnold was from somewhere else,
where it was warm; where he wore suede shoes
and played ping-pong.
Arnold knew the Koran.
And he knew to sing:
    Young Julien Sorel
    Knew his Latin well
    And was wise as he
    Was beautiful
    Until his head fell.

In the empty atmosphere
Arnold kept a tiplet pigeon, a bag of chicken corn.
He thought of Eleanor, her hands;
watched her sit sad in school
He got Carmine to lure her into the warm atmosphere;
he wanted to kiss her, live with her forever;
break her head with bargains.

Who is Arnold? Well,
I first saw him wear a black cap
covered with old Wilkie buttons. He was 13.
And afraid. But with a smile. And he was always
willing to walk you home, to meet your mother,
to tell her about Hester Street Park
about the cold bums there;
about the cold old Jewish ladies who sat,
hands folded, sad, keeping their faces
away from the old Jewish Home.
Arnold grew up with a knowledge of bookies
and chicken pluckers

And Arnold knew to sing:
    Dead now my 15th year
    F.D.R., whose smiling face
    Made evil the buck-toothed Imperialist,
    The moustached Aryan,
    The jut-jawed Caesar—
    Dead now, and I weep . . .
    For once I did hate that man
    and no reason
    but innocent hate
    —my cap decked with old Wilkie buttons.

Arnold was kicked in the balls
by an Italian girl who got mad
because there was a big coal strike on
and it forced the Educational Alliance to close its doors.
Arnold, weak and dying, stole pennies from the library,
but he also read about Paderewski.
He used to walk along South Street
wondering about the various kinds of glue.
And it was about airplane glue he was thinking
when he fell and died beneath the Brooklyn Bridge.

ITALIAN EXTRAVAGANZA

Mrs. Lombardi's month-old son is dead.
I saw it in Rizzo's funeral parlor,
A small purplish wrinkled head.

They've just finished having high mass for it,
They're coming out now
. . . wow, such a small coffin!
And ten black cadillacs to haul it in.

BIRTHPLACE REVISITED

I stand in the dark light in the dark street
and look up at my window, I was born there.
The lights are on; other people are moving about.
I am with raincoat; cigarette in mouth,
hat over eye, hand on gat.
I cross the street and enter the building.
The garbage cans haven't stopped smelling.
I walk up the first flight; Dirty Ears
aims a knife at me . . .
I pump him full of lost watches.

EASTSIDE INCIDENTS

Aside from ashcans & halljohns & pigeoncoops
there were the sad backyards
the hot July stoops
There were those mad Valenti kids who killed my cat
with an umbrella
There was Dirty Myra who screwed the Rabbi's son
in the cellar
And there was Vito & Tony & Robby & Rocco
I see them now
eating poisoned mushrooms and vomiting air
killing Mr. Bloom the storekeeper
and getting the chair
I see them now
but they aren't there

WRIT ON THE EVE OF MY 32ND BIRTHDAY

a slow thoughtful spontaneous poem

I am 32 years old
and finally I look my age, if not more.
Is it a good face what's no more a boy's face?
It seems fatter. And my hair,
it's stopped being curly. Is my nose big?
The lips are the same.
And the eyes, ah the eyes get better all the time.
32 and no wife, no baby; no baby hurts,
    but there's lots of time.
I don't act silly any more.
And because of it I have to hear from so-called friends:
"You've changed. You used to be so crazy so great."
They are not comfortable with me when I'm serious.

Let them go to the Radio City Music Hall.
32; saw all of Europe, met millions of people;
        was great for some, terrible for others.
I remember my 31st year when I cried:
"To think I may have to go another 31 years!"
I don't feel that way this birthday.
I feel I want to be wise with white hair in a tall library
        in a deep chair by a fireplace.
Another year in which I stole nothing.
8 years now and haven't stole a thing!
I stopped stealing!
But I still lie at times,
and still am shameless yet ashamed when it comes
        to asking for money.

32 years old and four hard real funny sad bad wonderful
        books of poetry
—the world owes me a million dollars.

I think I had a pretty weird 32 years.
And it weren't up to me, none of it.
No choice of two roads; if there were,
        I don't doubt I'd have chosen both.
I like to think *chance* had it I play the bell.
The clue, perhaps, is in my unabashed declaration:
"I'm good example there's such a thing as called soul."
I love poetry because it makes me love
        and presents me life.
And of all the fires that die in me,
there's one burns like the sun;
it might not make day my personal life,
        my association with people,
        or my behavior toward society,
but it does tell me my soul has a shadow.

Victor Hernández Cruz

VICTOR HERNÁNDEZ CRUZ WRITES: *On the day of my birth, half of the Town of Aguas Buenas, Puerto Rico, was in my house drinking hot chocolate and eating crackers. There was no hospital for miles. Aguas Buenas is a small town toward the interior of Puerto Rico. It is surrounded by guava trees and is protected by* Los Santos Reyes (*The Three Kings*). *Aguas Buenas demanded its independence from Caguas, a larger town that sits next to it and of which it was once a part. It became a* municipio *in 1838. My grandfather on my mother's side was fond of reciting poetry in the town plaza and he always had to be taken home drunk and singing a song. In the mornings it was good soup* (dc fideo) *for him and off to work in* el chinchal (*cigar shop*) *where he worked forming tobacco into the cigars for which Aguas Buenas was famous.*

While my father was serving in the U.S. Army he must've heard rumors about some place called New York. By the time I was four years old his curiosity got really strong and he went out ahead to scout the place out. A few months after his departure my mother, my sister, my aunt and myself were off to the capital to board a plane to New York. It took eight hours of flying time and my mother tells me that I cried all the way.

Our address was no longer Calle Muñoz Rivera
                                Aguas Buenas, Puerto Rico
It was 635 East 11th Street
     Apt. 12
     New York, New York
Years later the very house and spot that I was born in became a combination grocery store and bar with one of the loudest juke boxes in the Caribbean.

You are chosen to be a receiver of messages. From where? From everywhere, the room next door forms a different galaxy. I have a good memory and use it as a warehouse of words, stor-

ies, concerns for my work. The form takes shape itself without me thinking about it, I have no time to think about poetry when I am doing it. If you don't believe in something you won't see it, some people spend a great deal of time staring into the darkness waiting to see spirits and moving things and they never see anything because they only believe in everything happening through them and for them. . . .

Victor Hernández Cruz was born in 1949 and is the author of SNAPS (1969) and MAINLAND (1973).

POEM

The greater cities are
surrounded by woods
Jungles secretly
of America

Behind lights
the green
Green eyes of Tree gods
Rhythm we would call it Puerto Rico
But it doesn't begin to be as real

Silver of the moon
On the upper Hudson
Green Quiet night
Night island wish
Outside the stars
get fatter and louder
Secret jungle where
the moon is closer
Highway to the skies
Secret
Outside getting cold
We talk to the wind

That moves the world
before it becomes foul
Over the heads of
the buildings

We take it in our mouths
Drunk outside great

Electrical Apple / Nueva York
No Puerto Rico
Nueva York
No Puerto Rico/

TO THE SPIRIT OF CARLOS GARDEL

Songs of tears
Gallons of rum to
drown your fears
Generation of madness
Millions of children
were born that year
They are my fathers
My mothers
Listening now
To the old 78's
Streams of thought
Invade the faces
They open
And Carlos Gardel
Sways out
With his tango
His tango
That kept everybody
In love.

ENERGY

is
red beans
ray barretto
banging away
steam out the
radio
the five-stair
steps
is mofongo
cuchifrito stand
outside down
the avenue
that long hill
of a block
before the train
is pacheco
playing with
bleeding
blue lips

THE GROUP

all thru last
year they sang
& nothing happened
cept the ceiling
almost fell down
one day
& water came down
by the stairs
& the cops came &
took the grass.

so chup chup
bu ra
singing was going
to be life
& they could have
taken planes
all over
& ate lemons when
they got rusty

instead
they went to
jail.

AFRICAN THINGS

o the wonder man   rides his space ship/
                                    brings his power through
many moons
                carries in soft blood   african spirits
dance & sing in my mother's house. in my cousin's house.
black as night can be/   what was Puerto Rican all about.
                                            all about the
indios & you better believe it the african things
                                        black & shiny
grandmother speak to me & tell me of african things
                                    how do latin
boo-ga-loo sound   like you
                        conga drums in the islands you know
the traveling through many moons
                    dance & tell me black african things
i know you know.

BRONXOMANIA

snake horse stops at bronx clouds
end of lines and tall windowed cement
comes to unpaved roads and wilderness
where the city is far
and spanish bakeries sell hot bread
the roar of the iron snake
plunges at closing doorways
down fifty blocks
is the island of Puerto Rico.

LOS NEW YORKS

In the news that sails through the air
Like the shaking seeds of maracas
I find you out

Suena

You don't have to move here
Just stand on the corner
Everything will pass you by
Like a merry-go-round the red
bricks will swing past your eyes
They will melt
So   old
will move out by themselves

Suena

I present you the tall skyscrapers
as merely huge palm trees with lights

Suena

The roaring of the trains is a fast
guaguanco
dance of the ages

Suena

Snow falls
Coconut chips galore
Take the train to Caguas
and the bus is only ten cents
to Aguas Buenas

Suena

A tropical wave settled here
And it is pulling the sun
with a romp
No one knows what to do

Suena

I am going home now
I am settled there with my fruits
Everything tastes good today
Even the ones that are grown here
Taste like they're from outer space
Walk y Suena
Do it strange
Los New Yorks.

MEGALOPOLIS

*(megalopolis—is urban sprawl—as from
Boston to N.Y.C., Philly, Washington,
D.C., the cities run into each other)*

highway of blood/volkswagens crushed up
against trees
it's a nice highway, ain't it, man
colorful/it'll take you there
will get there round eight with corns on
your ass   from sitting
turn the radio on & listen/   no
turn the shit off
let those lights & trees & rocks
talk/ going by / go by   just sit
back/ we / go into towns/   sailing the
east coast / westside drive   far-off
buildings look like castles / the kind
dracula flies out of / new england of houses
& fresh butter / you are leaving the nice
section now   no more woods / into rundown
overpopulated areas, low income/ concrete walls
of america / a poet trying to start riots /
arrested with bombs in pockets / conspiracy
to destroy america/ america / united states /
such a simple thing/ lawrence welk-reader's
digest ladies news big hair styles with all
that spray to hold it/ billboards of the high-
way are singing lies / & as we sail we under-
stand things better / the night of the buildings
we overhead flying by/ singing magic words
of our ancestors.

Nicholas Flocos

Nicholas Flocos was born in Pittsburgh in 1930 of Greek parents. His father, now deceased, came to the United States at the turn of the century when he was twelve. "He came to work, of course, and to help out relatives in the old country. This was standard procedure. It was also standard procedure to return and marry, which he did after he received an engineering degree from Carnegie Institute of Technology in Pittsburgh."

Nicholas Flocos was educated at the University of Pittsburgh and at Columbia University. He lives in Pittsburgh, where he works for a large corporation and teaches an evening writing class at the University of Pittsburgh. His work has appeared in literary magazines and a collection of his poems, DUST COMES TO SWEET PIANOS, was published in 1974.

NICHOLAS FLOCOS WRITES: *I enjoy the written word more than the spoken word, and I like poetry because it justifies the hard work that writing is. I don't consider myself an ethnic in writing, although some poems do reflect an interest in where my parents (and my wife) came from. I like to read poetry and think it ought to be a habit developed by all who like to read anything, newspapers, magazines, etc. William Carlos Williams' lines say it nicely: "It is difficult to get the news from poems yet men die miserably every day for lack of what is found there."*

COIN FROM B.C.

The silver tetradrachm of King Antigonos
Will outlast us all, of course.
Oxidation and abrasion
Will do us in, as we expect,
Being usable coin.

Only the tales we hear and tell will last
As the silver tetradrachm of King Antigonos,
Which goes unspent at the market,
Though it could buy most anything.

ALLEGIANCE TO APHRODITE

Death makes me love you,
Sweet double-natured daughter
Of the greatest open secret:
Life's everlasting irony.

Death makes me love you
As sun whitens the snow,
As men lash cuttle-fish against
The rock to make them tender.

Death makes me love you
As sun reddens the rose,
As mockingbird rises to Olympus
But heads on to find the sea.

GOSSIP

In the mountains of the Peloponnesus,
The bus rest-stopped in a dusty town;
I do not recall its name, only its effect
On our morale.   We got out and stretched
And breathed.   "Here is where . . ." someone said;
Something about the wing-heeled Hermes, about
His having been less than a clean-cut messenger:
The kind of news that does a quick circle.

When we got back on, what Hermes had allegedly
Done there was like yeast through us.
We sat fatter in our seats and more comfortably.

Tourists of the classical, we had not been drawn
So close by any Praxiteles or ruin in all Arcadia.
O how we admired that fast Olympian as we looked
Out at his trees and saw our vaulting selves.

THE OLD UPRIGHT I DID NOT LEARN TO PLAY

Strange how our failures shine in memory;
As if dust comes only to sweet pianos.

The old upright I did not learn to play
Stands highly varnished in a corner of my mind,
The blue silk shawl on its top triangularly
Apexed downward to the clean ivory keyboard
Where each Monday afternoon at four-thirty
I failed with illiterate fingers.

The shawl shimmers brightly in retrospect;
The piano, as if attuned to victory,
Glows like a trophy brought out into sunlight,
And awarded to Music for withstanding Inability.

BOGART

I grew up on Humphrey Bogart movies; it was like church.
I liked the way he would look tired muscles at wickedness
And smoke cigarettes existentially, better than Europeans.
"To Have and Have Not" was what his eyes always said;
No matter what the picture was (Queeg as well as The Downer

Of the Drink to Forget Ingrid) the Great Rub was there:
That to have was not to have and not to have was to have.
He granulated that Rub till I could sprinkle it on toast;
In a big feast scene he would see to it that I, a cult of one
In the middle row, got the right feeling for the leftovers;
His empathy was like a nun's, it fed on eternals and grit.
Good wouldn't always win so much as grandeur would,
Grandeur as seen from the squinting empathetic eye he was.

GARDEN BLOOMS

Hyacinth

It is the Greek waiter
Of the garden. Egalitarian
Without elbows.   It madams and sirs.
Quakes occur inside it
But outside nothing stirs.

Sweet William

By any other name than this:
Dianthus barbatus.
A mini-apocalypse,
Eurasian pink and spotted,
Looks princely best
In plural, potted.

Sunflower

The tycoon of flowers speaks
Through monied sunburst cheeks:
Helianthus is the name;
Producing oil's my game.

SALT

Old smiling woman, you have had all the lessons
and now you sit in black on the high front porch
amused by the rough diamonds who have not had.
Your eyes seem to sally with epigrams.
You sit as if long ago you were sold to an opponent
and through sufferance supernal became wiser than he,
and more artful and blithe. And less embarrassed.

Old smiling woman, having had all the lessons,
you sit as if you could be Punchinello's grandmother
and know exactly what mistake he will make next.
You sit as if all the murmuring, beautiful world
decided by vote that because of your good salt,
you should be the one to look down from that porch
and repeat *Kyrie Eleison* in that learned black dress.

COMFORT FROM ARCADIA

Nobody ever told my grandmother Eleni
That Arcadia is all in the mind.
She sent me chamomile from its glens
To comfort stomach-ache and sniffles.
She persisted in mailing letters
To America postmarked Arcadia
As if there were such a place
To send letters from and chamomile.

My poor old grandmother Eleni
Did not know the secret about Arcadia's
Being a pipedream of Pan's.
To the very end she thought
She lived there and even invited me
To visit her and pat her goat Vasili

Which had a bell on a red ribbon
Around its neck that told her
She was not really alone.
Her last letter said poor Vasili
Was her only comfort but was getting old.

IN THE GAZEBO

In the evenings the old country old take
their placid gaits and Panamas up Wood Street.
Retired, they have given what they had to give.

Now Wilkinsburg treats them to a roundhouse perch
to hear the Seventies simmer and watch the sandaled
apostle-haired young of this new country.

New when they came here fifty and sixty years
before, it is new again.   Once more these men are
immigrants in wrong hats on Wood Street.

Their lapels wrong again too, their ties too slim
now instead of too wide, they sit in the town's
new redwood gazebo, amazed once more at America.

Pocket watches gone, wrists turn up Bulova time,
their last modernity.   Out-clocked, they sit in on this new
country: old country men with two old countries now.

Sam Hamod

Hamode Samuel Hamod was born of Lebanese-Muslim parents in their boardinghouse on 3rd and Jefferson streets in Gary, Indiana, February, 1936. "My earliest recollections are of my father, mother and maternal grandfather, plus a lot of guys who roomed at the hotel and ate with us—gandy dancers, railroad firemen and engineers, open-hearth workers—everything —and from every nationality in the world."

After receiving his B.S. from Northwestern, Sam Hamod entered and then dropped out of the University of Chicago Law School and returned to Gary to open a tavern in the Black section. "A roughhouse type of place, but big and fast, and I had B.B. King and Muddy Waters play on weekends. Even old Redd Foxx told his dirty jokes there. But it got to be too much hassle, so I went back and earned an M.A., then began teaching in universities. During this time I also did some traveling in and over the world, got married and had two children (David and Laura)."

He says his poetry didn't come alive until he attended the University of Iowa. "Anselm Hollo, Jack Marshall and some other friends believed in me, and after some crucial things happened in my life, some good poems came out on paper. Also, meeting David Kherdian, and hearing him talk through his big, black, bushy mustache—the meeting of the Arab poet with the Armenian poet—once again proved to me that my blood was an important source for my poetry. Then, with a little help from my friends, I pushed on and finally completed my Ph.D. in the Writer's Workshop and Center for Modern Letters in Iowa City."

Sam Hamod has published two full-length books of poetry, THE HOLDING ACTION (1969) and THE FAMOUS BOATING PARTY (1970). He is the editor of *Surviving in America,* a poetry journal, and the editor/publisher of Cedar Creek Press.

SAM HAMOD WRITES: *It seems a long way from Gary, yet it's not. My whole life stays with me, ever present: my grandfather and father, strong men who used to buy me bananas and take me down by the railroad to see the huge steam engines, men who believed in the American dream every immigrant has (while sending money home to support the rest of their tribe in Lebanon)—preaching Islam and working in the Mosques for their people; the strength of my mother to survive in this life; my first marriage and two children; the friends who have been found and lost along the way; Valparaiso; Iowa City; Sally (my present wife); Rock Falls, Wisconsin, and the farm, the Lunds, the Galeps, Brownie, Peg and the others who made the air so clear; Pennsylvania and the good few there; Anselm, Jack, David, Ken, Tom and Mac, good poets all; and the-old-Arab in-my-mind who is with me always—all these people, these things, stay with me and they keep talking, coming through with their faces and words, they come now like light, showing me the ways I have gone, ways I go, and are parts of the ways I shall go.*

LINES TO MY FATHER

My Father is watching over his Mosque, silently
He hovers now, praying;
My Father is sitting on the step watching,
Holding his chest where the bullet entered his prayer,
Holding on, the maple trees blurring in his eyes,
He cannot rise, he is praying as his blood comes,
My Father is planting maple trees beside his Mosque,
     digging each hole
Carefully, patiently knowing the trees will grow,
He is watering the grass outside his Mosque at 3 a.m.,
His work is done and now my Father is covering the grass
     with love.

My Father is moving East, to Leb'nan, eating kib'be, his
Mother offering him grapes and shade,
He is walking in the mountains, drinking water;
My Father is sitting on a park bench beside me
Taking the air, watching my children in the grass,
He is talking of water,
He is trying to rest
But he must go, his Mosque is waiting.
My Father, dreaming of water when wakened,
when I found him, had only blood in his mouth.

THE FIGHT

My Grandfather
the Hajj Abbass Habhab
one late afternoon
wrapped a chair
around the neck
of one hillbilly
named Gene
closed another around Fred
from Knoxville
and had Nik
the Hungarian
in a head-
lock,
all this
after
they jumped
him
in the kitchen
of my old
man's hotel
3rd and Jefferson   Gary, Indiana

1940   Christmas
day   they were
all drunk except
my Grandfather the Hajj
Abbass, who
never drank but
loved
to shovel coal
and fight

THE FAMOUS HOT PEPPER EATING CONTEST

There's my old man
with Nik the Hungarian   both of them standing there
having their hot-pepper-eating-contest
each of them choosing a redder pepper and Mexican Chili's
        by the handful
biting in,   chewing until their faces turn red and their
        eyes water
holding on in my dreams   they keep chewing out there
        in the garden
for years now they've been doing this
never once letting up

THE LOSS OF BLACK CAMELS

It seems there should be someplace in a poem for black camels
especially since I've never seen any, they should make good
        symbols
or at least a good metaphor or be combinable into a decent
        simile
(similes however are a drag and metaphors wear thin after
        you figure them)
so we throw them away—goodbye black camels,   goodbye
        goodbye

MOTHER'S DAY

My Mother came again,   her
Gray hair still full of sorrows;
She is slowing down,
The light is further away—spaces extend
Into distances as she talks, but they close
When I feel her eyes,   I would reach her
But I am never deep enough,   though I do not
Fear depths,   I move in her darkness,   then somehow,
We join in our losses,   my Mother and I,
Hoping for a better next time

LEAVES

Tonight Sally and I are making stuffed grapeleaves
we get out a package that is drying out.
I've been saving them in the freezer, it's one
of the last things my father ever picked in this life.
They're over five years old
and up to now
we just kept finding them in the freezer
as if he were still picking grapeleaves somewhere,
packing them carefully to send to us
making sure they don't break.
"To my Dar Garnchildn
Davd and Lura
from Thr Jido"
twisted on the paper
in this English lettering hard for him to even print.
I keep this small torn record
this piece of paper stays in the upstairs storage
one of the few pieces of American my father ever wrote,
but we find his Arabic letters all over the place, even have
a letter from Charles Atlas telling him that in 1932,

"of course, Mr. Hamod, you can build your muscles like
     mine . . ."
and last week my mother told me,   "Yes, your father also
made up poems, didn't you remember him singing in the car
when we drove"   even now
at night, I sometimes get out the Arabic grammar book,
though it seems so late

AFTER THE FUNERAL OF ASSAM HAMADY

(for my mother, David and Laura)

cast:

Hajj Abbass Habhab: my grandfather
Sine Hussin: an old friend of my father
Hussein Hamod Subh: my old man
me

6 p.m.

middle of South Dakota
after a funeral in Sioux Falls
my father and grandfather
ministered the Muslim burial
of their old friend, Assam Hamady

me—driving the 1950 Lincoln
ninety miles an hour

"STOP! STOP
stop this car!"

Why?

"STOP THIS CAR RIGHT NOW!"—Hajj Abbass
                              grabbing my arm from back seat

"Hysht Iyat? (What're you yelling about?)"—my old man
"Shu bikkee? (What's happening?)"—Sine Hussin

I stop

"It's time to pray"—the Hajj
                    yanks his Navajo blanket
                    opening the door

"It's time to pray, sullee
the sun sets
time for sullee"

my old man and Sine Hussin follow
obedient
I'm sitting behind the wheel
watching, my motor still running

car lights scream by
more than I've ever seen in South Dakota

the Hajj spreads the blanket
blessing it as a prayer rug
they discuss which direction is East

after a few minutes it's decided
it must be that way
they face what must surely be South

they face their East, then notice
I'm not with them

"Hamode! get over here, to pray!"

No, I'll watch
and stand guard

"Guard from what—get over here!"

I get out of the car
but don't go to the blanket

My father says to the others:
"He's foolish, he doesn't know how
to pray."

they rub their hands
then their faces
rub their hands then
down their bodies
as if in ablution
their feet bare
together now
they begin singing

Three old men
chanting the Qur'an in the middle
of a South Dakota night
    "Allahu Ahkbar
    Allahu Ahkbar

    Ash haduu n lah illah illilawhh
    Ash haduu n lah illah illilawhh

    Muhammed rasoul illawh"

in high strained voices they chant

    "Bismee lahee
    a rah'manee raheem"

more cars flash by

    "malik a youm a deen
    ehde nuseerota el mustakeem
    seyrota la theena"

I'm embarrassed to be with them

    "en umta aliy him
    ghyrug mughthubee aliy him"

people stream by, an old woman strains a gawk at them

"willathouu leen—
    Bismee lahee"

I'm standing guard now

  "a rah'maneel raheem
    khul hu wahu lahu uhud"

They're chanting with more vigor now
against the cars—washing away
in a dry state
Hamady's death

he floats from their mouths
wrapped in white

  "Allahu sumud
    lum yuulud wa'alum uulud"

striped across his chest, with green

  "willa thouu leen"

his head in white, his grey mustache still

  "Ameen . . ."

I hear them still singing now
as I travel half-way across
America
to another job
burying my dead
I always liked trips, traveling at high speed
but they have surely passed me
as I am standing here now
trying so hard to join them
on that old prayer blanket—
as if the pain behind my eyes
could be absolution

Joy Harjo

Joy Harjo was born May 9, 1951. Her father is a Creek Indian. "We are from Oklahoma—Alabama originally, before removal in the 1830s." She was born in Tulsa, Oklahoma, and was graduated from the high school of the Institute of American Indian Arts in Santa Fe, New Mexico. She attended the University of New Mexico in Albuquerque, where she was an art major studying painting, on a Bureau of Indian Affairs Scholarship.

Joy Harjo is divorced and the mother of two children. The poems published here are her first to appear in a book.

JOY HARJO WRITES: *My writing has something to do with roots. Words come through me, which means through my mother and father, through their mothers and fathers. . . . These are roots, and these are where I am from.*

THE LOST WEEKEND BAR

The Lost Weekend bar
   in Tahlequah Okla.
is no place to be
   on Monday nights.
Too many ghosts
   come out
from the Illinois River
   drinking their way
uptown,
   across the courthouse lawn,
inside
   the tavern
to wet old bones
   and dried livers.
They stay;
   they are the last to go home.

At daylight,
    you can see them stumbling
back down
    to the Illinois River.

CREEK MOTHER POEM

her long brown fingers
must have trembled
in her dying
when she touched you
her three day old son
who lay crying
in her long black hair

it was just three days
when they put her in the grave
her breasts cold
but quivering full of milk

her long brown fingers
must have trembled

LAME DEER

he must be coyote
            ma'ii
seeker of visions
old man
thousands of years old
it must have been you
i saw

sometime ago
outside of that
South Dakota bar
in the middle of winter
making tracks
like coyote
                wine stains
                in the snow

just barely made it home
that time
                didn't you?

IGNACIO, COLORADO   FOR YOU THAT TIME

Albuquerque Indian militants
                                ha
we were protecting
the Southern Ute tribe
                                brothers
drinking with them
for three days
we never came out of
                the Teepee Lounge

have a drink, brother
Sam passed out a little ways
just this side of Cuba

SNAKE POEM I

snake   climbs
   on flat rocks
sways   sliding
   his body hugs
each niche   closely
   taking the rock color
   blending
becoming that rock
 until sun moves
  and cool shadows
   are too cold
    for snake; the weaver
weaving rocks and the sun

(A HOPI WOMAN TALKING)

she told me
(her hands moving)
of the twin eagles
they kept at first mesa

and how they were named
in the morning
after being washed
with water and cornmeal
and blessed with
an ear of mother corn

she said then
(her hands moving)
how tame they were
(and called their names)

and said how they
were smothered
and their feathers were taken
with praying
and they were buried
at dawn

that's what she told me
this morning

THE PEOPLE

There is a man walking
tall between the mountains
He has been walking for
three hundred thousand years
He has marked the earth
many times
with the trail of his feet
He walks in four directions
making a circle
always a beginning
He is singing
between the mountains:

        the people
        hey-yah
        the land
        hey-yah-ah
        the mother
                hey-yah

He walks singing
for three hundred thousand years.

Lawson Fusao Inada

Lawson Fusao Inada is a sansei (third generation Japanese-American), born in Fresno, California, in 1938. His father's people come from Kumamoto; his mother's from the samurai clan of Wakayama, and it was her father, Busuke Saito, who started the Fresno Fish Store, a famous West Side landmark. During the Second World War Lawson Fusao Inada lived with his family in "relocation camps" in Fresno, Arkansas and Colorado.

After the war they returned to the multi-ethnic West Side, where he attended high school. Not a Buddhist, he became part of the Black and Chicano scene. "The main thing then was music: Johnny Ace, Augustin Lara, Little Walter, etc., and on into Lester Young and Charlie Parker. They made me want to 'say' something."

Lawson Fusao Inada is married and has two boys. The four Inadas live in Ashland, Oregon, where he teaches in the English Department of Southern Oregon College.

He is Co-Editor of AIIIEEEE!: AN INTRODUCTION TO ASIAN AMERICAN WRITING (1974), and the author of BEFORE THE WAR: POEMS AS THEY HAPPENED (1971), which deals with his experiences in relocation camps during the war. In 1972 he received a writing fellowship from the National Endowment for the Arts.

LAWSON FUSAO INADA WRITES: *Welcome to Murrka, son. As an Asian-American writer, one of the very few, I must think in terms of being a social historian, a social force, one who speaks of who we are. There are over a million of us on the reservation, and we've been here for seven generations. Welcome to Murrka, son.*

ASIAN BROTHER, ASIAN SISTER

For Yoshiko Saito

I.

Not yet dawn,
but the neighbors have been here,
bringing condolences, assurances
that my pupils will be seen to:

though I am new to their village
they include me, are grateful
for what I do.

The teacups are rinsed.
The bedding is stacked.
While my wife wraps our basket
the children kneel on the tatami,
fingering the beads of the rosary like an abacus.
In their way, they are hushed,
and seem to sense the solemnity.

"Sa. Iki-ma-sho."

A cold wind greets us.
There will be snow soon
in this prefecture.

Burnt wood, sweet fields.
Not yet dawn.
In one of these houses,
my grandmother is rising to go to school.

II.

By sixteen,
she was in this country—

making a living, children
on the way.

I don't know what it cost
in passage, in the San Joaquin.

I'm beginning
to understand the conditions.

III.

To get back to the source,
through doors

of dialects and restrictions . . .

Brazil to the south, this blue
shore on the horizon . . .

To get back to the source,
the need to leave

and bring it with you:

in 1912, they opened
the Fresno Fish Store.

IV.

Ika, the squid,
to slither down your throat.

Saba, the mackerel,
to roast.

Maguro, the tuna—
slice it thin and raw.

Kani, the crab.
Awabi, the abalone.

All these
shipped in slick and shiney.

All these
to keep our seasons.

All these.

V.

Grandmother never learned the language—
just a few
choice phrases to take care of business.
Grandfather ordered the fish.

But when the nice white man
bent down to her level and said
"How long you been here, Mama?"
she told him
"Come today fresh."

VI.

Before the war, after
the old scrape of stench and scale,
she'd come to see what her new grandson could do.

Nine o'clock, but you've got to wake him,
so I can flip him in his crib.

Bring him down to the store tomorrow
so I can get him some manju,
let him chew on an ebi.

Part his hair in the middle,
slick it down,
so I can wheel him around to the people.

Listen, big baby—Mexican tunes
moving around the jukeboxes.
Listen, big fat round-headed baby in white shoes.

What chu mean
he's got small eyes?
What chu mean?
That's how he
supposed to be.
What chu mean?
Big fat baby in a hood.

In depths of bed,
to roll to where the shore was, undulating
coves and folds . . .

Drunks dancing wounded
under a wounded streetlight . . .

Then the Danish Creamery
screaming about its business
and we couldn't sleep.

Sing me. Sing me. Sing me
please about the pigeons
cooing home to the temple to roost.

Sing me. Please.

For our sweet tooth,
she kept a store
of canned fruit buried in the dirt
beside her barracks in Arkansas.

51 / LAWSON FUSAO INADA

Water flopping over the furo's edges
as we entered, feet
sliding on slats,
a soft iceberg in the heat and steam . . .

So you've got a son in New Guinea,
another at some fort.
What do you do?
What have you *been* doing?—

try to keep busy and eat.

And as the children leave
to dicker with the enemy,
try to keep busy and eat.

Float around him,
bump and nudge him,
and try to keep busy and eat.

Shuffle off to the store
ten feet behind him
and try to keep busy and eat.

And when the sons take over,
try to keep busy and eat.

Go in and scream about the business.
Grandchildren stumbling
over their own skin in the suburbs,
hubcaps and money
cluttering the driveways . . .

One day they found her
flipping in a driveway like a fish.

If your hip is broken,
you can't ever go home—
roaming through Wakayama
for what the War didn't own.

If your hip is broken,
you can't ever go to Oregon.
You've got to wheel to your drawer
for your Issei medallion—

that steamer riding a starry-striped sea.

If your hip is broken,
you've got to give that medallion
with a moan—

as though you could know.

VII.

My grandmother is in the beauty
of release.
As the heart subsides,
as the blood runs its course,
she is gowned and attended,
chanting incantations to Buddha.

I am touched by the beauty,
by the peace
that is the end of her life—

fluttering eyelids,
the murmuring barely audible.

It is goodbye.

It is beautiful.

I do not need to cry.

As the sheet flows over in its purity,
I note the smoothness
of skin, the grey-blue hair
echoed faintly over the lips.

Then the sheet becomes a paper bag,
and she slips out of that sack
off the kitchen table

and lands on her back
on the linoleum,

naked, moaning, the impact
having stunned her into fright.

And she grabs both legs of mine
and bends the knees
and brings me down upon her

blue mouth without teeth,
food beginning to swell
in her belly.

where I am

crying, and not yet born.

VIII.

This house. This house.
The paths become trenches to the telephone, the bathroom . . .
This house. The scent of Orient
and seven existences.

This house. The bedrooms
tacked-on then sealed-off
as each moved to the colonies.

This house. Fifty years in this house.
Lie in front of the heater and dream,
flames eating the snowflake
mica that shudder with color
like fish-scales—blue, red—dream . . .

Lie in front of this heater
and knead the pus
where fish-fins stuck,
your dreams a fish
wilting over this heater . . .

This house. Creamery and cleavers
going at each other down the wintery street.

Bitches in alleys,
bottles in dreams . . .

Who knew the black whore in the alley
of this house—
dead a week, wrapped in leaves . . .

Tread lightly in this house.
Appliances try the edge of trenches.
Grandchildren balance on the shelves—
tassled
offspring of another culture . . .

This house. The basement
crammed with ballast—
dolls, kimonoes, swords . . .

This house. That survived the War
and got stoned.
This house. Exhausted fumes

gnawing the garden on the shore.

In the mist of that shore,
the chrysanthemum
droops and nods.

This house.

It drops into the freeway
and I drown.

IX.

Then the doors burst open
and the people come flooding in—

from all over the San Joaquin
come to form the procession.

There is a trench to the temple.

When you are in that trench,
there is no room
for much movement:

all that you move from
comes in on you;
all that you do
is judged upon.

Trapped in the trench,
I am smothered in my people,
chanting in procession to the temple.

And when we emerge in the temple
I am five feet two,
flat-faced, bent-legged, epicanthic
as I will ever be . . .

Do my eyes lie?

My people see I am beautiful.

Yes. I am rocked in the lap of Buddha.
Yes. Incense owns my clothes.
Yes. I am wrapped in beads.

Yes. My people.
Grandmother, take me in your arms.

What you say, I will do.

x.
The procession continues . . .
My grandfather migrates
to my mother's house, in the suburbs.
Even the chrysanthemum
finds new root, in the suburbs.

I have the medallion
forever sailing on my breast—
a family and the seven gods of luck
in the hold.

Brothers, Sisters,
understand this:

you are in passage—
wherever you go
you are slanted
down to the bone.

Do your eyes lie?

Brothers, Sisters,
understand this:

you are beautiful.

And your beautiful grandmother
is dancing in your eyes,

cooing and cooing you
home to roost.

David Kherdian

David Kherdian was born on December 17, 1931, in Racine, Wisconsin, of Armenian parents who had fled the Turkish Massacres at the turn of the century. He explains that the culture within the culture in his hometown was Armenian, and that the Armenians in the diaspora believed that their only hope was to refound the race by founding new families. "They came in great numbers, mainly peasants from Kharpet, because there was available work in the factories and cheap labor was in demand. They literally worked themselves to death, and while I knew at a very early age that I would have to carry the burden of their sacrifice all my life, I also knew that I would not do so by following in their footsteps."

For nineteen years, between the ages of nineteen and thirty-eight, David Kherdian was "on the move—the army & college & Europe & an endless series of odd jobs: unloading boxcars, shoe clerking, magazine selling, rug merchanting, office help, book scouting—and always, secretly, scribbling: waiting for the stuff to become good enough to spring on the world." He has also worked as a literary and library consultant, magazine editor and college teacher, and has been the official poet-in-the-schools for the state of New Hampshire.

He is the author of SIX SAN FRANCISCO POETS (1969), as well as ON THE DEATH OF MY FATHER AND OTHER POEMS (1970), HOMAGE TO ADANA (1971), LOOKING OVER HILLS (1972), A DAVID KHERDIAN SAMPLER (1974), a selection from his published poetry, and THE NONNY POEMS (1974). He lives with his author/artist wife, Nonny Hogrogian, in a hamlet on a trout stream in upstate New York, where he writes, reads, daydreams and fishes for trout.

DAVID KHERDIAN WRITES: *At the age of 4½ my mother enrolled me in nursery school so I could learn my first foreign language—English. Sometime soon after that I learned that my country of origin was America, not Armenia, and I went all out in an American way to be what I had naturally been all along—a native son;—that is, until my late 20s, when my Armenian blood reclaimed me. Since then I have worked my way through race, nationality, region, and all other ties but family, to stand as my own man, responsible to myself and my chosen commitments.*

MY MOTHER TAKES MY WIFE'S SIDE

This is an
ignominious tale about the naming
of a family of which I am a member.
Our name, I must (reluctantly)
confess, is Turkish, and occurred
so long ago that our true Armenian
name has been lost—perhaps forever.

One early evening, in an unknown year
of our Lord, one of my forefathers—
(a maker of doors;—a carpenter) went
to a Turk's home to collect on the
door he had made him.

The Turk wouldn't be bothered and
slammed the door of the door-
maker into the door-maker's face,
WHEREUPON,
enraged in a fury that is so
common to Armenians but
as puzzling to *odars*
as their behavior is puzzling to us,
broke the door in two
and fled.

"*Kherda khatchda*," the Turk exclaimed, or
kherda (broke), *khatchda* (run).

The name stuck.

And what may seem
a casual incident for the naming of
such a name is not,
for the name couldn't have been more
accurate, or the mood in which the
action took place more fitting,
for the Kherdians have always been,
and are still,
impulsive and crazy—
        "a little touched"
we used to say as kids—

An expression that recalls my father.

And this afternoon
in discussing marriages and the faults
of men with my mother, and after she
had denounced every male that we had
moved into the conversation,
I asked with an innocence I enjoy
affecting:

"And what is my fault as a husband?"

"You ask that!" she shouts, "after
storming out of the house yesterday,
leaving your wife with tears in her face!
Your crazy Armenian temper is your fault!
Need it be asked? Must it be told?"

"*Kherda khatchda*," I say, smiling.

"Pot kut," my mother replies in Turkish,
two words of another meaning
better designed to describe
this particular Kherdian.

TO MY SISTER

Pa would often have to fetch you home.
Crouched, withdrawn, certain your way
must be explored alone;
leaving for a morning or an afternoon,
often to see the moon on the lake at night,
or the sun's first color and beginning light.
But he was your father,
who left his young moods in another land
and turned to you with his love
a buffoon and a man.

We were all strangers: all shy, reclusive
and alone. We never found a healing grace,
who couldn't mate this soil with our lives.
A family is a strange thing when a living
racial embrace has been broken and the
earth or the world are no longer home.
It is a private peace we have made,
each in his own way, though we shared
one home, in this country that would never
be home.

I seem to recall a stooped and aging man,
crippled in one leg from a fall;
bald, and hardly taller than a young
girl's height. And you beside him
reluctant of the hand you held.

Nothing in this life has ever again
been as strange as this picture
I either remember or seem to have known.

DTAH DTAH

Seated on a metal folding chair
    long afternoons
    in front of the church
An old nameless Armenian man
    anonymous except for nationality
    and a secret bond
    between God and countrymen.
Sundays he became a part of the throng
    and shuffled quietly inside
    always out of sight
But all week he held this mysterious vigil
    in old clothes
    and beatific smile.
Strange how men for whom I held
    a secret pity then
    were really the guardians
    of a way of life
    and life itself.

MY MOTHER AND THE AMERICANS

My mother, who
sees life at that
peculiarly oblique angle
that is commonly referred to
as artistic insight,
is the visionary poet
of the family,

            but fortunately,
(for those disciples who
hope to succeed her),
she doesn't practice her arts
outside the home

and one day,
looking out the window into
memory and the future,
she announced:
            "These Americans raise
their children like chickens—
            Any which way."

UNITED STATES TONY

United States Tony
was such a man
that amused factory workers
on the home-going bus
by dancing in the aisle
while another man sang;

Never able
to let life lie
one day he invited
his Armenian friend
to a theft of pears
from a farmer's orchard
on the way to the Cudahy Fair;

Promptly caught and challenged
he laughingly replied
(circling the tree
and clapping his hands)

No! No! You can't arrest
me, I'm United States Tony;
No! No! You can't arrest me,
I'm United States Tony;

That aura he carried
circled and danced
and went with him
all the places he went;

And true to the prediction
he had made in the past
he died before drawing
his first pension check;

And died with his name
and his life intact.

MY FATHER

My father always carried a different
look and smell into the house when he
returned from the coffee houses in Racine.
Playing in the streets we would stop,
walk quietly by, and peer in thru the
cracked doors at the hunched backgammon
players, their Turkish cups at their elbows.

Years later, reading the solemn and bittersweet
stories of our Armenian writer in California,
who visited as a paperboy coffee houses in
Fresno, I came to understand that in these
cafes were contained the suffering and
shattered hopes of my orphaned people.

UMBAJI PARK

for Avak Akgulian

Sloping at a 45° angle
and cut into a triangle
in the shadow of St. Patrick's
Church on Erie Street, from
which it took its official
name, Umbaji, the old
Armenian bachelor, sat in
his park.

In one corner a drinking
fountain that gave white
water falling on bright
pebbles that sparkled white
and brown, and then a fence
and thick shrub bushes and
a cement wall along one side,
by the sidewalk, so the children
wouldn't fall down.

Old folks and bums and just
plain people came single file
and sat on the one bench that
Umbaji was said never to leave,
and it went on being known, by
children and Armenians, as
Umbaji Park.

The fountain is broken and gives
only enough water for dogs and
mad children; the shrubs gone,
the fence rusted, the grass worn
and belonging only to nature,

whose spring rains feed it, whose
winter snows cover it, and the
bench and Umbaji are forever gone.

And so it has, maybe because of
all this, or maybe because the old
man is no longer there, a worn, carefree,
dogged and useless look; for this is
its spirit: neither defunct nor dead,
but tired and confused, because the
old man is no longer there to hold
it all together with his presence and
his love.

Something there died when he did,
and kept others from resurrecting
what was his alone, and so Umbaji
is there still, haunting his park in
death as in life, carrying his bench
under his arm, sitting in corners we
cannot see, still the lonely inhabitant
in the only home he was ever given, or
could make, or could call his own.

Charles Reznikoff

Charles Reznikoff was born in Brooklyn, New York, on August 31, 1894. He spent a year at the School of Journalism of the University of Missouri, and in 1915 received his L.L.B. from the Law School of New York University. He was admitted to the Bar of the State of New York the following year but did not practice law because he was primarily interested in writing He married author/editor Marie Syrkin in 1930 and they make their home in Manhattan, where he has lived most of his life.

Charles Reznikoff is the author of a number of volumes of verse and several volumes of prose. BY THE WATERS OF MANHATTAN, a selection of his verse, appeared in 1962 and the next year the Jewish Book Council of America gave him their award for poetry in English. He was awarded the Morton Dauwen Zabel Award for Poetry by the National Institute of Arts and Letters in 1971. BY THE WELL OF LIVING AND SEEING was published by the Black Sparrow Press in 1974.

CHARLES REZNIKOFF WRITES: *"Objectivist," images clear but the feeling not stated but suggested by the objective details and the music of the verse; words pithy and plain; without the artifice of regular meters; themes, chiefly Jewish, American, urban.*

From FIVE GROUPS OF VERSE (1927)

4

How shall we mourn you who are killed and wasted,
sure that you would not die with your work unended,
as if the iron scythe in the grass stops for a flower?

17

Ghetto Funeral

Followed by his lodge, shabby men stumbling over the
    cobblestones,
and his children, faces red and ugly with tears, eyes
    and eyelids red,
in the black coffin in the black hearse the old man.

No longer secretly grieving
that his children are not strong enough to go the way
    he wanted to go
and was not strong enough.

18

Showing a torn sleeve, with stiff and shaking fingers
    the old man
pulls off a bit of the baked apple, shiny with sugar,
eating with reverence food, the great comforter.

29

A Citizen

I know little about bushes and trees,
I have met them in backyards and streets;
I shall become disreputable if I hang about them.
Yet to see them comforts me,
when I think of my life as snarled.
Was not knowledge first on trees?

32

How difficult for me is Hebrew:
even the Hebrew for *mother*, for *bread*, for *sun*
is foreign. How far have I been exiled, Zion.

33

God saw Adam in a town
without flowers and trees and fields to look upon,
and so gave him Eve
to be all these.
There is no furniture for a room
like a beautiful woman.

35

After I had worked all day at what I earn my living,
I was tired. Now my own work has lost another day,
I thought, but began slowly,
and slowly my strength came back to me.
Surely, the tide comes in twice a day.

36

Samuel

All day I am before the altar
and at night sleep beside it;
I think in psalms, my mind a psalter.
I sit in the temple. From inside it
I see the smoke eddy in the wind;
now and then a leaf will ride it
upward and when the leaf has spinned
its moment, the winds hide it.
Against their hurly-burly
I shut the window of my mind,
and the world at the winds' will,
find myself calm and still.

The days in this room become precious to others also,
as the seed hidden in the earth becomes a tree,
as the secret joy of the bride and her husband becomes a man.

Whatever unfriendly stars and comets do,
whatever stormy heavens are unfurled,
my spirit be like fire in this, too,
that all the straws and rubbish of the world
only feed its flame.

The seasons change.
That is change enough.
Chance planted me beside a stream of water;
content, I serve the land,
whoever lives here and whoever passes.

From SEPARATE WAY (1936)

13

Kaddish

"Upon Israel and upon the Rabbis, and upon their disciples and upon all the disciples of their disciples, and upon all who engage in the study of the Torah in this place and in every place, unto them and unto you be abundant peace, grace, lovingkindness, mercy, long life, ample sustenance and salvation, from their Father who is in Heaven. And say ye Amen." Kaddish de Rabbanan, *translated by R. Travers Herford.*

Upon Israel and upon the rabbis
and upon the disciples and upon all the disciples of their
    disciples
and upon all who study the Torah in this place and in every
    place,
to them and to you
peace;

upon Israel and upon all who meet with unfriendly glances,
     sticks and stones and names—
on posters, in newspapers, or in books to last,
chalked on asphalt or in acid on glass,
shouted from a thousand thousand windows by radio;
who are pushed out of class-rooms and rushing trains,
whom the hundred hands of a mob strike,
and whom jailers strike with bunches of keys, with revolver
     butts;
to them and to you
in this place and in every place
safety;

upon Israel and upon all who live
as the sparrows of the streets
under the cornices of the houses of others,
and as rabbits
in the fields of strangers
on the grace of the seasons
and what the gleaners leave in the corners;
you children of the wind—
birds
that feed on the tree of knowledge
in this place and in every place,
to them and to you
a living;

upon Israel
and upon their children and upon all the children of their
     children
in this place and in every place,
to them and to you
life.

From GOING TO AND FRO AND
WALKING UP AND DOWN (1941)

26

Autobiography: Hollywood

I

I like the streets of New York City, where I was born,
better than these streets of palms.
No doubt, my father liked his village in Ukrainia
better than the streets of New York City;
and my grandfather the city and its synagogue,
where he once read aloud the holy books,
better than the village
in which he dickered in the market-place.

28

Kaddish

I

In her last sickness, my mother took my hand in hers
tightly: for the first time I knew
how calloused a hand it was, and how soft was mine.

II

Day after day you vomit the green sap of your life
and, wiping your lips with a paper napkin,
smile at me; and I smile back.
But, sometimes, as I talk calmly to others
I find that I have sighed—irrelevantly.

I pay my visit and, when the little we have to say is said,
go about my business and pleasures;
but you are lying these many weeks abed.
The sun comes out; the clouds are gone; the sky is blue;
the stars arise; the moon shines; and the sun shines anew
for me; but you are dying,
wiping the tears from your eyes—
secretly that I may go about my business and pleasures
while the sun shines and the stars rise.

IV

The wind that had been blowing yesterday has fallen;
now it is cold. The sun is shining behind the grove of trees
bare of every leaf (the trees no longer brown
as in autumn, but grayish—dead wood until the spring);
and in the withered grass the brown oak leaves are lying,
gray with frost.
"I was so sick but now—I think—am better."
Your voice, strangely deep, trembles;
your skin is ashen—
you seem a mother of us both, long dead.

V

The wind is crowding the waves down the river
to add their silver to the shimmering west.
The great work you did seems trifling now,
but you are tired. It is pleasant to close your eyes.
What is a street-light doing
so far from any street? That was the sun,
and now there is only darkness.

VI

Head sunken, eyes closed,
face pallid,
the bruised lips parted;
breathing heavily,
as if you had been climbing flights of stairs,
another flight of stairs—
and the heavy breathing
stopped.
The nurse came into the room silently
at the silence,
and felt your pulse,
and put your hand
beneath the covers,
and drew the covers to your chin,
and put a screen about your bed.
That was all:
you were dead.

VII

Her heavy braids, the long hair of which she had been proud,
cut off, the undertaker's rouge
on her cheeks and lips,
and her cheerful greeting
silenced.

VIII

My mother leaned above me
as when I was a child.
What had she come to tell me
from the grave?

Helpless,
I looked at her anguish;
lifted my hand
to stroke her cheek,
touched it and woke.

IX

Stele

Not, as you were lying, a basin beside your head
into which you kept vomiting; nor, as that afternoon,
when you followed the doctor slowly with hardly the
        strength to stand,
small and shrunken in your black coat;
but, as you half turned to me, before you went through the
        swinging door,
and lifted your hand, your face solemn and calm.

X

We looked at the light burning slowly before your picture
and looked away;
we thought of you as we talked but could not bring ourselves
        to speak—
to strangers who do not care, yes,
but not among ourselves.

XI

I know you do not mind
(if you mind at all)
that I do not pray for you
or burn a light
on the day of your death:
we do not need these trifles
between us—
prayers and words and lights.

Carolyn M. Rodgers

Carolyn M. Rodgers was born in Chicago, Illinois. Concerning her birth, she is willing to declare only that she is a Sagittarius. She received her formal education at the University of Illinois and Roosevelt University, where she majored in English and psychology. After college she worked as counselor and language arts instructor for high school dropouts. She left the field of social work to become a free-lance writer.

Her writing has won three awards: the first Conrad Kent Rivers Writing Award (1969), a National Endowment for the Arts Award (1970) and The Society of Midland Authors Award (1970). She is a member of OBAC (Organization of Black American Culture), and the Gwendolyn Brooks Writing Workshop. For a time, she was a columnist for the *Milwaukee Courier* and a book reviewer for the *Chicago Daily News*. She now spends her time writing and traveling around the country reading her poetry or lecturing on Afro-American Literature. Her talent is wide-ranging, and she has written memorable stories as well as important criticism.

Carolyn M. Rodgers' poems have appeared in numerous anthologies and her poems, stories and articles have been published in such national magazines as *Ebony* and *The Nation*. She has written two books of poetry, PAPER SOUL (1968) and SONGS OF A BLACKBIRD (1969).

CAROLYN M. RODGERS WRITES: *I grew up on the south side of Chicago. 47th Street. There, there were dirty pissy alleys and topless smelly garbage cans and backyards where trees grew and yielded Indian cigars. My parents were hard factory and steel mill workers. They went to church, prayed, saved money and sent all four of us, three girls and one boy, to college. In short, they prayed, fought and saved their way and our ways out of the many death traps of the black ghetto. I was a loner, more or less, as a kid. I loved to read and by the time I was nine*

I kept a diary. As a child, I thought my parents were too strict about where we could and could not go, but now I realize that they had a survival plan and there were rules to be followed. Anyhow, we had a big backyard and dogs, and almost every year until I was nearly twelve, mother and daddy let us (and all the other kids in the neighborhood who wanted to) try and dig a hole to Mexico.

JESUS WAS CRUCIFIED, or,
                    It Must be Deep
                        (an epic pome)

    i was sick
    and my motha called me
    tonight yeah, she did she
    sd she was sorri
    i was sick, but what
        she wanted tuh tell
    me was that i shud pray or
    have her (hunky) preacher
    pray for me. she sd. i
    had too much hate in me
    she sd u know the way yuh think is
    got a lots to do
    wid the way u feel, and i
    agreed, told her i WAS angry a lot THESE days
    and maybe my insides was too and she sd
        why it's somethin wrong wid yo mind girl
    that's what it is
                    and i sd yes, i was aware a lot
    lately and she sd if she had evah known educashun
    woulda mad me crazi, she woulda neva sent me to
    school (college that is)
    she sd the way i worked my fingers to the bone in

this white mans factori to make u a de-cent some-
bodi and here u are actin not like decent folks
          talkin bout hatin white folks & revolution
& such and runnin round wid NegroEs
     WHO CURSE IN PUBLIC! ! ! ! (she sd)
THEY COMMUNIST GIRL! ! ! DON'T YUH KNOW THAT? ? ?
     DON'T YUH READ*THE NEWSPAPERS? ? ? ?
                                        (and i sd)
i don't believe—(and she sd) U DON'T BELIEVE IN GOD
                         NO MO DO U? ? ? ? ?
u wudn't raised that way! U gon die and go tuh HELL
and i sd i hoped it wudn't be NO HUNKIES there
and she sd
what do u mean, there is some good white people and some
bad ones, just like there is negroes
and i says i had neva seen ONE (wite good that is) but
she sd negroes ain't readi, i knows this and
deep in yo heart you do too and i sd yes u right
negroes ain't readi and she sd
why just the utha day i was in the store and there was
uh negro packin clerk put uh colored woman's ice cream
in her grocery bag widout wun of them "don't melt" bags
     and the colored ladi sd to the colored clerk
"how do u know mah ice cream ain't gon tuh melt befo I
git home."
               clerk sd. "i don't" and took the ice cream
               back out and put it in wun of them "stay hard"
               bags,
and me and that ladi sd see see, ne-groes don't treat
nobody right why that clerk packin groceries was un
grown main, acted mad. white folks wudn't treat yuh that
way. why when i went tuh the BANK the otha day to de-
posit some MONEY
this white man helped me fast and nice. u gon die girl
and go tuh hell if yuh hate white folks. i sd, me and

my friends could dig it. . . hell, that is
she sd du u pray? i sd sorta when i hear Coltrane and
she sd if yuh read yuh bible it'll show u read genesis
revelation and she couldn't remember the otha chapter
i should read but she sd what was in the Bible was
happnin now, fire & all and she sd just cause i didn't
    believe the bible don't make it not true
            (and i sd)
    just cause she believed the bible didn't make it true
and she sd it is it is and deep deep down
in yo heart u know it's true
            (and i sd)
    it must be d
        eeeep
she sd i mon pray fuh u tuh be saved. i sd thank yuh.
    but befo she hung up my motha sd
    well girl, if yuh need me call me
i hope we don't have to straighten the truth out no mo.
i sd i hoped we didn't too
        (it was 10 P.M. when she called)
she sd, i got tuh go so i can git up early tomorrow
and go tuh the social security board to clarify my
record cause i need my money.
work hard for 30 yrs. and they don't want tuh give me
$28.00 once every two weeks.
      i sd yeah. . .
don't let em nail u wid no technicalities
    git yo checks. . . (then i sd)

    catch yuh later on jesus, i mean motha!

    it must be
        deeeeep. . .

IT IS DEEP

(don't never forget the bridge
that you crossed over on)

Having tried to use the
witch cord
that erases the stretch of
thirty-three blocks
and tuning in the voice which
    woodenly stated that the
    talk box was "disconnected"

My mother, religiously girdled in
her god, slipped on some love, and
laid on my bell like a truck,
blew through my door warm wind from the south
concern making her gruff and tight-lipped
       and scared
that her "baby" was starving.
she, having learned, that disconnection results from
            non-payment of bill (s).
She did not
recognize the poster of the
grand le-roi (al) cat on the wall
had never even seen the book of
Black poems that I have written
thinks that I am under the influence of
       communists
when I talk about Black as anything
other than something ugly to kill it befo it grows
    in any impression she would not be
considered "relevant" or "Black"
                but
there she was, standing in my room
not loudly condemning that day and

not remembering that I grew hearing her
curse the factory where she "cut uh slave"
and the cheap j-boss wouldn't allow a union,
not remembering that I heard the tears when
they told her a high school diploma was not enough,
and here now, not able to understand, what she had
been forced to deny, still—

she pushed into my kitchen so
she could open my refrigerator to see
what I had to eat, and pressed fifty
bills in my hand saying "pay the talk bill and buy
some food; you got folks who care about you. . ."

My mother, religious-negro, proud of
having waded through a storm, is very obviously,
a sturdy Black bridge that I
crossed over, on.

A NON POEM ABOUT VIETNAM
or (Try Black)

1.

I have been asked to write a poem about
Vietnam. I have been asked to label my-
self, (as if I am a brandless jar), as "pro"
or "con", on the War.

2.

I have been coaxed to deliver an opinion
About our black boys who, though still so
young they forget to wipe the milk from
their mouths, are being flown in
silver super jets to hot dark swamps, to
fight spiked booby traps and other brown-skinned
powerless people.

3.

Someone has even asked me to elaborate on the
idea of a Black boy/man fighting for a red/
white & blue democracy. It is difficult to
separate the answers from my feelings and tears,
and record on paper anything that is waterless
or sane.
But I have been told to "deal with the question
sensibly."

4.

Therefore, I have summed up my sane/opinion/
comment/statement/using 50 words, or less—
It is this:

  "no black man (or negro) should fight the hunkie's
    war, cause everytime we kill a Vietnamese,
    we are widening the crack in our own behinds
    for the hunkie to shove his foot into."

I hope that this opinion/comment/statement
makes
my label clear.

TO THE WHITE CRITICS

my baby's face is a

short story, smooth—tight & tech/ni/cally

cor-rect.

my baby's tears are a three-act play, a sonnet, a novel,

a volume of poems.

83 / CAROLYN M. RODGERS

my baby's laugh is the point and view

a philosophical expression of

oppression and survival,

my baby's life is a high celebration

       and

a black procreation of

       universality.

GREEK CRAZEOLOGY

(*Note: Black fraternities & sororities are dedicated to partying and whitening the minds of their members. They seek to form an elite group of negroes who are supposedly better than other Black people, g.d.i.'s or goddamn independents they are called. What these niggers are doing is acting out the Black slave/white master syndrome. The pledge is the slave; the member, the white master (in their sick fantasy). The act of pledging is masochistic & sadistic and imitates perverted culture. Black people have no time for such nonsense. If the pledges and members would spend as much TIME & MONEY working for the r(evolution), we could possibly begin to move the way we need to, in order to SURVIVE.*)

Alphaomegadeltasigmakappazetassssss (sing-song fashion)

the ducks are quacking
the weeds of ivy are growing
the dogs are howling
the tics and worms are crawling
      Pledge! Pledge! Pledge!
pledge yoself to be a duck
pledge yoself to be a ivy weed
pledge yoself to be a dog
pledge yoself to be a tic or a worm
      Yeah Yeah Yeah Pledge! ! !
be a duckweeddogwormtictacneoshit

and when the r(evolution) flames
Black warriors will roast all the ducks
Burn all the weeds
Shoot all the dogs that be foaming death at the
mouth/mind with Black Truth Rabies shots
And all the tics and worms will be fed to the
garbage-eating pigs in the streets. Yeah. Pledge!
                    Pledge! ! !

Pledge . . . yoself . . . to . . . death.

   YEAH, I IS UH SHOOTIN OFF AT THE MOUTH, YEAH, I
IS UH FAIRY TALE OR YEAH, I IS UH REVOLUTIONIST!

i is uh revolutionist
i has uh blue newport dashiki
and uh solid gold tiki.
my girlfriend, she got uh natural
and i does too
my mother, she go tuh breadbasket
ev'ry sat. morning
and we is saving to buy as many
Black businesses as we can.
i is uh revolutionist
cause i don't eat pig no mo
cause i dun read Fanon &
Malcolm and i quote LeRoi &
Karenga & my brotha—he be-
long to the Black Panther
Party!
yeah, i is uh revolutionist
and i belongs to uh revolutionary
group What GOT FuNDED (!) (and we is got some guns)
and was tellin the wite folks (out in whatchamacallit)
what we was gon do tuh them.

i gives the fist everytime i
see uh brotha, i speak swa-
hili ½ % of the time and i
stay on the wite boys and
negroes case
i write poetry since day befo yesterday
and i use words like muthafucka & goddamn to show
that i'm bad—i listens to coltrane ev'ry morning
when i take my shower and i dream about sun-ra & the
cosmos. yeah, i is uh revolutionist, yeah YOU BET!
   i IS uH ReVoLuTioNiST! ! !
       BOOOOOOOOOOM

Ladies & Gentlemen—We are sorry to announce that
our REVOLUTIONIST for this week's
installment of AESOP'S FAIRY TALES
just shot his mouth off with
his tongue. . . . . . .
      3-3-69

Luís Omar Salinas

Luís Omar Salinas was born in Robstown, Texas, in 1937. "I grew up as a child in Catholic schools where I learned to tolerate hate, smoked little candy cigars and was creative in spirit and really full of fun."

Luís Omar Salinas lived in Mexico for several years, and then with his aunt and uncle in Bakersfield, California. After graduation from a local high school, he attended various California colleges, working his way through as a dishwasher, construction worker and newspaper reporter.

His poetry has appeared in literary magazines, in numerous anthologies and in a collection, CRAZY GYPSY, published in 1970. He is also a playwright.

LUÍS OMAR SALINAS WRITES: *I have no* rosinante *to ride but am traveling on my poetry to reach the stars, come ride with me, I hope not to fall on my ass.*

> *—And when we get to the stars*
> *we'll weave blankets for the poor*
> *help make rain*
> *and socialize equally*
> *with a breakfast of wind.*
> *And a mind full of light*
> *"explaining wisdom*
> *for the oppressed."*
>
> *Omar*

ODE TO MEXICAN EXPERIENCE

(*on a chateau, I slept after watching* . . .)

The nervous poet sings again
in his childhood voice, happy,
a lifetime of Mexican girls
in his belly/

The midnoon sound of bells
and excited mariachis
in those avenues persuaded out
of despair.

He talks of his Aztec mind
to those around him,
the little triumphs and schizoid trips
its depths of anguish
the many failures
and his defeated chums
dogs and shadows,
the popularity of swans in his neighborhood
and the toothaches of rabbits
in the maize fields.

I know you in bars,
in merchant shops,
in the roving eyes of gladiators
and their loved ones,
in boats of Mazatlán that never anchor,
in the smile of her eyes,
in the tattered clothes of school children,
in the never ending human burials:
those lives lost in the stars
and those lost in the wreckage
of fingernails,
the absurd sophistry of loneliness
in markets, in hardware stores,
in brothels.

The happy poet talks in his sleep,
the eyes of his loved one
pressing against him
her lips have the softness
of olives crushed by rain.

I can think of the quiet nights
in Monterey
and of my sister who woke me up
in the mornings.
The soft aggressive spiders
came out to play in the sunlight,
and suffering violins in pawn shops,
hell and heaven and murdered angels
and all the incense of the living
in poisoned rivers
wandering aimlessly amid dead fish,
dead dreams, dead songs.
Yes!
I was an altar boy,
a shoe shine boy,
an interventionist in family affairs,
a ruthless connoisseur of vegetables,
a football player.
To all living things I sing
the most terrible and magnificent
Ode to my ancestry.

TIHUITKLI

Tihuitkli
        you slew the python
then went off
        in your motorcycle
to buy a hamburger/
and nobody gave a damn
not even your grandmother
who raised you/
and now we see you

with your girl friends
talking about Plato
    and Kafka
wearing Levis
and going to movie houses/
Tihuitkli
    you are welcome
    here
but what are your
    people
going to say
when they see you
singing
    American songs
to the village girls?

SEÑOR TORRES

Señor Torres
You know
    I am Mestizo
and that I am poor/

why do you
cheat
    us
in the weighing
of our cotton?

Hasn't Choucuatl
told you
we planned
to kill you?

Your blood
on our cotton
will make
beautiful blankets.

HAPPINESS IS A CHARLIE
CHAPLIN MOVIE

Papa . . . here are the $7
I made picking cotton.
Give me a quarter
I want to go see Charlie Chaplin.

THIS IS NOT A POEM

Outside the cold, the rain, the happy dogs
and injured automobiles play with the scared
shadows and my ceaselessly brooding mind;
Cesar Chavez is in jail, my car is leaking oil,
bill collectors greet me at the door,
the house is a mess, my girl friend has pneumonia
and I am without a job.
But the gritos of Mexican music radiate from the house
and there is laughter even from my ancestors
who come out of their graves from time to time
to chide me from my laziness and poetry.
In my hometown, my little nephew refuses to take
a bath, his sister is chewing tobacco that looks
like candy, and my brother-in-law is working
overtime again.

91 / LUÍS OMAR SALINAS

Here in my house, my typewriter is neurotic,
the books I read are censored by catholics,
and it looks like it's going to rain all night.
In the bookstores, "Crazy Gypsy" sleeps lazily
on the bookshelves
and book reviewers are going crazy in Mexico City.
This is an ordinary day.

Past days have seen the statutory rape of mosquitos
clouds complaining about their low status in society,
and pornographic mermaids disrobing at
Fresno State College.
The doorbell is ringing, it must be Santa Claus
or Little Orphan Annie looking for a place to stay.
No! It is a mermaid.
With a baby in her arms, people around her, the Mayor,
the Police Chief, with a summons for non-support.
Man, how could a mermaid have a baby?
This must be a joke.

ODE TO A VIOLIN

Six lessons
in six weeks

I leave
you

on a bench
wounded

BAREFOOT

Forgive
my Sadness

I blame
        Tequila

and a Rose
without
Shoes

FOR THE WAITER AT JHONNY PAVLOVS

He sees the ocean
        hanging on its lips
        and calls out each day
for mermaids to greet him
and thinks of how to meet
        the day
with willingness/

this is the shadow
of the road
        on his fist,
and the backroads of payrolls
to be met each
        Wednesday/

How can I kill the pain
at my bedside
if roses don't give me
        those years of waiting
in depots, he says,

93   /   LUÍS OMAR SALINAS

or why is my salad stale
in the afternoons
and why do I think
        of bullfighters?/

he day dreams of turnips
and watches the faces
        of spiders move into
        the sun
and he thinks he'll convince
his grandmother/

but tomorrow will be Sunday
and he'll be asleep.

WHAT A WAY TO LOSE THE WAR

I must find a slut tonight
and pray for rain
in this god forsaken
        orchard ape desert/
no one complains
about this infernal hell
        but the farmers
who seldom take baths
to save water
                for their goddamn crops/
I understand this scandal
                    about and over lettuce
is making people
        sick in the stomach
so many not accustomed yet
                to saucy tamales

or militant complaints
                  about the national revenue.
I could care less
my stomach is like an iron
                  bucket
          and the linings
                        are political
and hot like demonstrations.
So be it. America!
How can you lose?

WHATS MY NAME IF NOT EVERYONE ELSES

Madness is my sidekick
and I see rainbows for doorways,
and on my wall
there are no faces;
so grieve a little
for yourself—
cause my lifes been made
by your sanity,
and the cause of my ills
are not yours—
so take a deep breath,
eat lemons
and smile in public
cause everyones looking at you—
and I'm just a Poet,
imperfect
but passionately
at odds with my environment.

Stephen Stepanchev

Stephen Stepanchev was born on January 30, 1915, in Mokrin, a village in the Banat region of Yugoslavia. His father, a farmer, died in 1920, and his mother decided to go to America for a few years to earn some money and then return. Her father was already in Chicago, working in an ice-manufacturing plant, and so, Stepanchev relates, "in 1922 my mother and I joined him. The stay proved to be permanent. While I attended the public schools of Chicago, my mother stitched buttonholes in men's vests by hand for such clothing manufacturers as Kuppenheimer and Hart, Schaffner & Marx. During the Depression of the 1930s my grandfather returned to his family in Romania and died there shortly after his return. My mother stayed on, sewing buttonholes in men's vests for thirty years.

"I attended the University of Chicago on a scholarship which I won by competitive examination and received an A.B. degree in 1937. I was elected to Phi Beta Kappa in the same year. In the following year I received an M.A. degree. For three years, from 1938 to 1941, I taught English at Purdue University. Then I was drafted into the U.S. Army and served for four years— through World War II. I rose in rank from private to first lieutenant. After the war I was an instructor in English at New York University and earned a Ph.D. in American Literature. Since 1949 I have been teaching at Queens College, where I am Professor of English."

Stephen Stepanchev has been writing poems since his grammar school days. His first important publication was a group of poems in the February, 1937, issue of *Poetry*. At the time he was still an undergraduate at the University of Chicago. These poems won the Midland Authors Prize, given by *Poetry* later that same year. Since then his work has appeared in numerous literary magazines, and he is the author of four books of poems —THREE PRIESTS IN APRIL (1956), SPRING IN THE HARBOR

(1967), A MAN RUNNING IN THE RAIN (1969) and THE MAD BOMBER (1972)—and of AMERICAN POETRY SINCE 1945: A CRITICAL SURVEY (1965).

STEPHEN STEPANCHEV WRITES: *For me, poetry is a form of meditation. I conjure up images of the world and study them for contrasts and resemblances. I join them in structures that are dramatic and emotional. I give them an appropriate rhythm. I put them in a phrase environment that is on the frontiers of language. Then I hope.*

IN SPLIT: DIOCLETIAN'S PALACE

The roots of ferns
Are defacing the walls of the palace.
They dig into the masonry, and it sifts down
Like sugar on my head.

It is evening,
And the owls, catching the moonlight,
Blink like lanterns.
There is a sound of fountains in the distance,
Like boys pissing.
History hangs from the roof of the cathedral
And the peristyle
And the ancient lusts of the bath.

My fathers loved this place,
Washing the flagstones with their blood,
Before they left for the steel mills
And more efficient slaughter-houses of Chicago.

BUYING LILIES

The sky walks into the florist's shop.
Lilies, lilacs, and tulips sing at the door.
Flames of soprano voices leap in the new light.
The owner smiles and offers me an Eden.

Drawn, I resist. Ten dollars is the price of lilies.
My mother fed a family of four
During the Depression on ten dollars a week.

But the green morning whispers like champagne.
I buy the trumpeting lilies and let them cry
In the blue vase on my white, corner book-case.

Now their scent mixes with the smell of sneakers,
Sweat-stained sweaters, and suppers of soup and bread.

IRONDALE

They work in an iron mill
And serve an iron machine.
They stir, they tap the cauldrons
Making rivers of steel.
They melt down in that steel;
Their burning lives melt down.

They soon forget the green
Village of green dances
Leaping on berry hills.
They soon forget the leaves,
Lambs, and falconry,
Father's green history.

At night they pour the slag
Down a hill of slag,
Brushing the sky with fire.
Dozens of cars on the road
Pause to watch their lives
Pouring out like gold.

TRAILING MY BALLOON

I did not know the laws of the land
Or the birds or shirts on the lines.
Trailing my balloon, I stared
Through needles of sun at my uncles, bare

And running to catch a pig in the mud,
Straining to give it a death-bed of straw.
I saw horned pig's feet torn by rope
And uncle elbows bleeding into law.

I held on tight to my balloon
When the horned knife cut fat-lady folds
At the pig's throat, quivering. The cry
Sandpapered through my ear and mind.

I held on tight when white smoke shook
From the crackling straw and my balloon
Bobbed and the pig's skin spurted oil.
I held on tight, and Uncle John,

Rolling his eyes, brought me a charred
Ear, sacramentally, to eat.
Dazed, I did no bull-work, rated
His smile glassy. Slowly, I ate.

I had learned already not to wipe away
My aunt's wet kiss and to smile at the rustling
Bush and my mother's gaming friends.
I ate all uncle day, a citizen.

VOYAGE

I stand on the wharf,
Waving the smoke
Of good-bye away.
Something distorts the scene.

You carry tons of baggage,
Your life,
To Romania.
Will the ship hold up?

A horn warns me
That this pain
Is some sort of punishment.

O Olga,
I am the smoke
Of an old fire
My father's match lit
In a darkness
That is with me still.

Love me, love me!

A horn warns me
There is more than glass
Between us
That we never touch.

My handkerchief
Pulls me
Back to the city.

A truck stands on the road,
Abandoned,
Its motor running.

THE ROADS

As night creates the sun, silence
Shapes whatever you say
Into song. The children run by,
Two by two, making a frieze.

There is a passage of shadow over the iron
Fence and a volley of wind in the yard.
The children are fishing with balloons for stars.
They carry a box of stars.

On the lake more stars are surfacing,
And I make my water-walk.

I will give you all of my roads.

THE HOLY EYE IS BLIND

When father climbed the tabooed tree and shook
Down apples with his hairy, reminiscent fist,
The man in the dark collected thunder and spoke,
Tumbling him among clocks, knives, and fanged fears.
A girl with an apple smiled away the years.

Warm rain and fever stirred the world's root down
The petalling centuries, and the wild eye shone
With lust even as flesh like rotted fabric fell
From the bones. But sons were always cozened; they marked
The thunder, the wind, and the dread eye in the dark.

Today the rioter wakes only drums of self
As he robs and rapes, for fear is the forest
Speaking or dead law. At last our kind
Is free to choose in its lonely, unroofed west,
And sons can contrive, for the holy eye is blind.

James Welch

James Welch, a Blackfeet Indian born in Browning, Montana, in 1940, lived in several parts of the Northwest during his early years. After graduating from high school in Minneapolis, he attended the University of Minnesota and Northern Montana College in Havre, Montana. After two years of working at odd jobs in various places, he completed his undergraduate studies at the University of Montana and then worked in the Master of Fine Arts program there, concentrating on creative writing. He has been writing ever since. James Welch is married and lives in Upper Rattlesnake, Missoula, Montana.

His poems have appeared in numerous literary magazines, including *The New Yorker, Poetry* and *New American Review,* and his first full-length book of poems, RIDING THE EARTHBOY 40, was published in 1971. He recently completed a novel about reservation life, titled WINTER IN THE BLOOD.

JAMES WELCH WRITES: *I have attempted in most of these poems to combine the mythical (sometimes creating my own myths out of half-remembered stories) with the present realities of reservation life. Sometimes I think the mythical Indian is more real to Americans than the reservation Indian because the reservations are generally out of the way and quiet. I hope these poems serve to remind people that Indians are still here.*

THE MAN FROM WASHINGTON

The end came easy for most of us.
Packed away in our crude beginnings
in some far corner of a flat world,
we didn't expect much more
than firewood and buffalo robes
to keep us warm. The man came down,

a slouching dwarf with rainwater eyes,
and spoke to us. He promised
that life would go on as usual,
that treaties would be signed, and everyone—
man, woman and child—would be inoculated
against a world in which we had no part,
a world of money, promise and disease.

BLACKFEET, BLOOD AND PIEGAN HUNTERS

If we raced a century over hills
that ended years before, people couldn't
say our run was simply poverty or promise
for a better end. We ended sometime
back in recollections of glory, myths
that meant the hunters meant a lot
to starving wives and bad painters.

Let glory go the way of all sad things.
Children need a myth that tells them be alive,
forget the hair that made you Blood, the blood
the buffalo left, once for meat, before
other hunters gifted land with lead for hides.

Comfortable we drink and string together stories
of white buffalo, medicine men who promised
and delivered horrible cures for hunger,
lovely tales of war and white men massacres.
Meaning gone, we dance for pennies now,
our feet jangling dust that hides the bones
of sainted Indians. Look away and we are gone.
Look back. Tracks are there, a little faint,
our song strong enough for headstrong hunters
who look ahead to one more kill.

CHRISTMAS COMES TO MOCCASIN FLAT

Christmas comes like this: Wise men
unhurried, candles bought on credit (poor price
for calves), warriors face down in wine sleep.
Winds cheat to pull heat from smoke.

Friends sit in chinked cabins, stare out
plastic windows and wait for commodities.
Charlie Blackbird, twenty miles from church
and bar, stabs his fire with flint.

When drunks drain radiators for love
or need, chiefs eat snow and talk of change,
an urge to laugh pounding their ribs.
Elk play games in high country.

Medicine Woman, clay pipe and twist tobacco,
calls each blizzard by name and predicts
five o'clock by spitting at her television.
Children lean into her breath to beg a story:

Something about honor and passion,
warriors back with meat and song,
a peculiar evening star, quick vision of birth.
Blackbird feeds his fire. Outside, a quick 30 below.

THE VERSATILE HISTORIAN

I came through autumn forests needing
wind that needed fire. Sun on larch,
fir, the ponderosa told me to forget
the friends I needed years ago.
Sky is all the rage in country steeped
in lore, the troubled Indians wise within
their graves. The chanting clouds

crowded against the lowest peak. I sang
of trouble to the north. Sleeping weasels robbed
my song of real words. Everywhere, rhythm raged.
Sun beneath my feet, I became
the statue needing friends in wind
that needed fire, mountains to bang against.

SURVIVING

The day-long cold hard rain drove
like sun through all the cedar sky
we had that late fall. We huddled
close as cows before the bellied stove.
Told stories. Blackbird cleared his mind,
thought of things he'd left behind, spoke:

"Oftentimes, when sun was easy in my bones,
I dreamed of ways to make this land."
We envied eagles easy in their range.
"That thin girl, old cook's kid, stripped naked
for a coke or two and cooked her special stew
round back of the mess tent Sundays."
Sparrows skittered through the black brush.

That night the moon slipped a notch, hung
black for just a second, just long enough
for wet black things to sneak away our cache
of meat. To stay alive this way, it's hard. . . .

PLEA TO THOSE WHO MATTER

You don't know I pretend my dumb.
My songs often wise, my bells could chase
the snow across these whistle-black plains.
Celebrate. The days are grim. Call your winds
to blast these bundled streets and patronize
my past of poverty and 4-day feasts.

Don't ignore me. I'll build my face a different way,
a way to make you know that I am no longer
proud, my name not strong enough to stand alone.
If I lie and say you took me for a friend,
patched together in my thin bones,
will you help me be cunning and noisy as the wind?

I have plans to burn my drum, move out
and civilize this hair. See my nose? I smash it
straight for you. These teeth? I scrub my teeth
away with stones. I know you help me now I matter.
And I—I come to you, head down, bleeding from my smile,
happy for the snow clean hands of you, my friends.

HARLEM, MONTANA:
JUST OFF THE RESERVATION

We need no runners here. Booze is law
and all the Indians drink in the best tavern.
Money is free if you're poor enough.
Disgusted, busted whites are running
for office in this town. The constable,
a local farmer, plants the jail with wild
raven-haired stiffs who beg just one more drink.

107 / JAMES WELCH

One drunk, a former Methodist, becomes a saint
in the Indian church, bugs the plaster man
on the cross with snakes. If his knuckles broke,
he'd see those women wail the graves goodbye.

Goodbye, goodbye, Harlem on the rocks,
so bigoted, you forget the latest joke,
so lonely, you'd welcome a battalion of Turks
to rule your women. What you don't know,
what you will never know or want to learn—
Turks aren't white. Turks are olive, unwelcome
alive in any town. Turks would use
your one dingy park to declare a need for loot.
Turks say bring it, step quickly, lay down and dead.

Here we are when men were nice. This photo, hung
in the New England Hotel lobby, shows them nicer
than pie, agreeable to the warring bands of redskins
who demanded protection money for the price of food.
Now, only Hutterites out north are nice. We hate
them. They are tough and their crops are always good.
We accuse them of idiocy and believe their belief all wrong.

Harlem, your hotel is overnamed, your children
are raggedy-assed but you go on, survive
the bad food from the two cafes and peddle
your hate for the wild who bring you money.
When you die, if you die, will you remember
the three young bucks who shot the grocery up,
locked themselves in and cried for days, we're rich,
help us, oh God, we're rich.

GOING TO REMAKE THIS WORLD

Morning and the snow might fall forever.
I keep busy. I watch the yellow dogs
chase creeping cars filled with Indians
on their way to the tribal office.
Grateful trees tickle the busy underside
of our snow-fat sky. My mind is right,
I think, and you will come today
for sure, this day when the snow falls.

From my window, I see bundled Doris Horseman,
black in the blowing snow, her raving son,
Horace, too busy counting flakes to hide his face.
He doesn't know. He kicks my dog
and glares at me, too dumb to thank the men
who keep him on relief and his mama drunk.

My radio reminds me that Hawaii calls
every afternoon at two. Moose Jaw is overcast,
twelve below and blowing. Some people . . .
Listen: if you do not come this day, today
of all days, there is another time
when breeze is tropic and riffs the green sap
forever up these crooked cottonwoods. Sometimes,
you know, the snow never falls forever.

SPRING FOR ALL SEASONS

Let the sloughs back up and history
will claim that lakes were here
and Indians poled their way from Asia
past monsoons and puddled heat of carp.
We know better. We know this land
wouldn't bring a dime for rain in China.

Practice your grin when clouds are red,
sky falls blue against the buttes.
Morning brings flood to verbena, planted
by some fool who thinks July forgets
the past. Our past is ritual,
cattle marching one way to remembered mud.

Bring on the fools. Let some sap declare
a ten year rain, a Japanese current
to carry us west to rain forests or east
or south and down. Eskimos are planting
corn where lunar waves crawl the ice,
snow, the Arctic desert gone.

CALL TO ARMS

We spoke like public saints
to the people assembled in the square.
Our gestures swayed the morning light
and bathed the town in public guilt.

All the weather poured down that hour
our lips witched the ears of thousands.
Whiny kids broke from their mother's arms,
charged the fields, armed with sticks.

Men wept and women clutched their steaming
heads and beat the savage mildness
from their hearts. The eyes were with us,
every one, and we were with the storm.

We rode out that night, our ponchos slick
and battered down against our thighs.
Our horses knew the way. None looked behind,
but heard the mindless suck of savage booted feet.

THE RENEGADE WANTS WORDS

We died in Zortman on a Sunday
in the square, beneath sky so blue
the eagles spoke in foreign tongues.
Our deeds were numbered: burning homes,
stealing women, wine and gold.

No one spoke of our good side,
those times we fed the hulking idiot,
mapped these plains with sticks
and flint, drove herds of bison wild
for meat and legend. We expected

no gratitude, no mercy on our heads.
But a word—the way we rode
naked across these burning hills.
Perhaps spring breakup made us move
and trust in stars. Ice, not will,

made our women ice. We burned
homes for heat, painted our bodies
in blood. Who can talk revenge?
Were we wild for wanting men to listen
to the earth, to plant only by moons?

In Zortman on a Sunday we died.
No bells, no man in black
to tell us where we failed.
Makeshift hangman, our necks,
noon and the eagles—not one good word.

Al Young

Al Young was born May 31, 1939 in Ocean Springs, Mississippi, son of Albert James, a professional musician and auto worker, and Mary (Campbell) Young.

He has worked as a professional musician, playing guitar and flute, and singing throughout the United States. He has also been employed as a writing instructor, disk jockey and language consultant. He married free-lance artist Arline Belch in 1963, and was graduated from the University of California, Berkeley, in 1969. In addition to music and literature, Al Young has avocational interests in mythology, popular culture and mysticism.

Al Young writes fiction as well as poetry. About his novel SNAKES, he said he had ". . . hoped to capture some of the more elusive and lyrical rhythms and melodies of Afro-American speech, a language that has only recently begun to be studied and appreciated seriously." In addition to SNAKES (1970), he has published another novel, WHERE IS ANGELINA? (1974), and two books of poems, DANCING (1969) and THE SONG TURNING BACK INTO ITSELF (1971), and he is the recipient of several poetry awards. He lectures at the Creative Writing Center, Stanford University, Stanford, California.

AL YOUNG WRITES: *Besides being as necessary as food, water, air, sunlight and sleep—poetry is my way of celebrating Spirit, in all of its infinite forms (charted and uncharted) as the central unifying force in Creation.*

THE DANCER

When white people speak of being uptight
theyre talking about dissolution & deflection
but when black people say uptight
they mean everything's all right.
I'm all right.

The poem brushes gayly past me
on its way toward completion,
things exploding in the background
a new sun
in a new sky
cantaloupes & watermelon for breakfast
in the Flamingo Motel
with cousin Inez
her brown face stretching & tightening
to keep control of the situation,
pretty Indian cheeks
cold black wavelets of hair,
her boyfriend
smiling from his suit.
We discuss concentration camps
& the end of time.
My mustache
wet with cantaloupe juice
would probably singe
faster than the rest of me
like the feathers of a bird over flame
in final solution of
the Amurkan problem.
Ah, Allah,
that thou hast not forsaken me
is proven by the light
playing around the plastic slats
of half-shut venetian blinds
rattling in this room on time
in this hemisphere on fire.
The descendants of slaves
brush their teeth
adorn themselves before mirrors
speak of peace & of living kindness &
touch one another

intuitively & in open understanding.
"It could be the end of the world,"
she says, "they use to didnt be afraid
of us but now that they are
what choice do they have
but to try & kill us?"
but she laughs & I laugh & he laughs
& the calmness in their eyes
reaches me finally
as I dig my spoon into the belly of a melon

A DANCE FOR MILITANT DILETTANTES

No one's going to read
or take you seriously,
a hip friend advises,
until you start coming down on them
like the black poet you truly are
& ink in lots of black in your poems
soul is not enough
you need real color
shining out of real skin
nappy snaggly afro hair
baby grow up & dig on *that*!

You got to learn to put in about
stone black fists
coming up against white jaws
& red blood splashing
down those fabled wine & urine-
stained hallways
black bombs blasting out real white estate
the sky itself black with what's to come:
final holocaust
the settling up

Dont nobody want no nice nigger no more
these honkies man that put out
these books & things
they want an angry splib

a furious nigrah
they dont want no bourgeois woogie
they want them a militant nigger
in a fiji haircut fresh out of some secret boot camp
with a bad book in one hand
& molotov cocktail in the other
subject to turn up at one of their conferences
or soirees
& shake the shit out of them

A DANCE FOR MA RAINEY

I'm going to be just like you, Ma
Rainey this monday morning
clouds puffing up out of my head
like those balloons
that float above the faces of white people
in the funnypapers

I'm going to hover in the corners
of the world, Ma
& sing from the bottom of hell
up to the tops of high heaven
& send out scratchless waves of yellow
& brown & that basic black honey
misery

I'm going to cry so sweet
& so low
& so dangerous,
Ma,

that the message is going to reach you
back in 1922
where you shimmer
snaggle-toothed
perfumed &
powdered
in your bauble beads
hair pressed & tied back
throbbing with that sick pain
I know
& hide so well
that pain that blues
jives the world with
aching to be heard
that downness
that bottomlessness
first felt by some stolen delta nigger
swamped under with redblooded american agony;
reduced to the sheer shit
of existence
that bred
& battered us all,
Ma,
the beautiful people
our beautiful brave black people
who no longer need to jazz
or sing to themselves in murderous vibrations
or play the veins of their strong tender arms
with needles
to prove that we're still here

TRIBUTE

Yes brothers you invented jazz
& now I'm inventing myself
as lean & prone to deviance
as the brilliance of your
musical utterance, a wind
that sweeps again & again
thru my American window

What a life you sent me
running out into expecting
everyone to know at once
just what it was I was
talking or not talking about

The genius of our race
has far from run its course
& if the rhythms & melody
I lay down this long street
to paradise arent concrete
enough it can only be because
lately Ive grown used to taking
a cozier route than that of
my contemporary ancestors

Where you once walked or ran
or railroaded your way thru
I now fly, caressing the sturdy
air with balls of my feet
flapping my arms & zeroing

LONESOME IN THE COUNTRY

How much of me is sandwiches radio beer?
How much pizza & neon messages?
I take thoughtful journeys to supermarkets,
philosophize about the newest good movie,
camp out at magazine racks & on floors,
catch humanity leering back in laundromats,
invent shortcuts by the quarter hour

There's meaning to all this itemization
& I'd do well to look for it in woodpiles
& in hills & springs & trees in the woods
instead of staying in my shack all the time
thinking too much,
                         falling asleep in old chairs

All those childhood years spent in farmhouses
& I still cant tell one bush from another—
Straight wilderness would wipe me out
faster than cancer from smoking cigarettes

My country friends are out all day long
stomping thru the woods all big-eyed &
that's me walking the road afternoons,
head in some book,
                         all that hilly sweetness wasting

                         Late January
                         Sonoma Mountain Road
                         in the Year of the Dragon

DANCING IN THE STREET

for my NYC
summer workshop
students

Just because you wear a natural baby
dont mean you aint got a processed mind.
The field is open
the whole circle of life
is ours for the jumping into,
we ourselves the way we feel
right now
re-creating ourselves
to suit particular dreams & visions
that are no one else's.

Who needs that big mortgaged house
those household finance cars
they advertise
so *scientifically*
between newscasts,
expensive fronts
those foot-long cigarettes
that brand of breath?

I'd have to travel all the way
back to Lemuria
(cradle of the race
beneath the Pacific)
to bring back a more golden picture of us
the way we looked today
the way we are all the time inside,
healthy black masters
of our own destiny;
set at last on slashing the reins

& shaking off the blinders
that keep the north american
trillion dollar mule team
dragging its collective ass
into that nowhere desert
of bleached white bones & bomb tests.

Notes

MEI BERSSENBRUGGE

Hieronymus Bosch. Dutch painter (1450?–1516)

Bhaudanath. The ancient Buddhist stupa in Bhauda, Nepal, described by the poet as having "a gold spire and painted eyes that stared at me in my mud house across the rice fields."

Bell and dorje. Tibetan symbols for male and female powers. The dorje, or thunderbolt, is the male.

VICTOR HERNÁNDEZ CRUZ

Carlos Gardel. A famous Argentinian tango singer

Ray Barretto. A Puerto Rican Conga player well known in the jazz and Latin American music world

Mofongo. A very tasty Caribbean dish made with plantains

Cuchifrito. Fried pork parts

Pacheco. Refers to Johnny Pacheco, a flautist from Santo Domingo who popularized the pachanga in the 1950s

Maracas. An indigenous rhythm instrument made from gourds or from the fruit of the higuera plant. It is dried and seeds are placed inside it.

Suena. Spanish verb meaning "sounds"

Guaguanco. A musical form created in Cuba with roots in Africa

NICHOLAS FLOCOS

Punchinello. A short, humpbacked clown or buffoon in Italian puppet shows

Kyrie Eleison. The brief prayer "Lord, have mercy," in the liturgy of the Greek Orthodox Church

JOY HARJO

Ma'ii. Navajo word for coyote

Murrka. America

Tatami. A bamboo mat

Sa. Iki-ma-sho. "Well. Let us go."

Manju. Sweet bean and rice cakes

Ebi. Shrimp

Issei medallion. In 1969, medallions, commemorating the cen-
tonniary annivorsary of tho Japanese in America, were
presented to surviving first-generation Japanese-Americans
—Issei—by the Japanese American Citizens League.

DAVID KHERDIAN

Odar. Non-Armenian

Pot kut. English equivalent: bull in a china shop

Dtah Dtah. Grandpa

CHARLES REZNIKOFF

Kaddish. Aramaic word meaning "holy" or "consecrated." In
Judaism, a prayer of praise to God; in present-day syna-
gogue liturgy it is also said as a mourner's prayer.

LUÍS OMAR SALINAS

Rosinante. The name of Don Quixote's bony old horse

Mestizo. A Spanish word meaning "half-caste"; specifically, in
Spanish America, a person of mixed Spanish and Ameri-
can Indian blood. Often used as another word for Mexican.

Cesar Chavez. Mexican-American labor leader who organized
Mexican agricultural workers

Gritos. Cheers usually used during a fiesta

AL YOUNG

Amurkan. American

Index to Titles

Index to First Lines